At Sylvan, we believe that everyone can master math skills, and we are glad you have chosen our resources to help your children experience the joy of mathematics as they build crucial reasoning skills. We know that time spent reinforcing lessons learned in school will contribute to understanding and mastery.

Success in math requires more than just memorizing basic facts and algorithms; it also requires children to make connections between the real world and math concepts in order to solve problems. Successful problem solvers will be ready for the challenges of mathematics as they advance to more complex topics and encounter new problems both in school and at home.

We use a research-based, step-by-step process in teaching math at Sylvan that includes thought-provoking math problems and activities. As students increase their success as problem solvers, they become more confident. With increasing confidence, students build even more success. The design of the Sylvan workbooks lays out a roadmap for mathematical learning that is designed to lead your child to success in school.

We're excited to partner with you to support the development of confident, successful, and independent learners!

The Sylvan Team

4th Grade Basic Math Success Workbook

Published in the United States by Random House, Inc., New York, and in Canada by Random House of Canada Limited, Toronto.

This book was previously published with the title *4th Grade Basic Math Success* as a trade paperback by Sylvan Learning, Inc., an imprint of Penguin Random House LLC, in 2010.

www.sylvanlearning.com

Created by Smarterville Productions LLC
Producer & Editorial Direction: The Linguistic Edge
Producer: TJ Trochlil McGreevy
Writer: Amy Kraft
Cover and Interior Illustrations: Tim Goldman and Duendes del Sur
Cover Design: Suzanne Lee
Layout and Art Direction: SunDried Penguin
Director of Product Development: Russell Ginns

First Edition

ISBN: 978-0-375-43042-8

Library of Congress Cataloging-in-Publication Data available upon request.

This book is available at special discounts for bulk purchases for sales promotions or premiums.
For more information, write to Special Markets/Premium Sales, 1745 Broadway, MD 6-2,
New York, New York 10019 or e-mail specialmarkets@randomhouse.com.

PRINTED IN CHINA

10 9 8 7 6

Contents

Number Words

WRITE the number words for each number.

HINT: Commas make big numbers easier to read. A comma belongs after the millions place and after the thousands place in both the number and its written form.

Example: **3,694,527**

3,000,000	three million
600,000	six hundred thousand
90,000	ninety thousand
4,000	four thousand
500	five hundred
20	twenty
7	seven

3,694,527 in written form is three million, six hundred ninety-four thousand, five hundred twenty-seven.

1. 2,439 two thousand, four hundred thirty-nine ____________________

2. 41,582 ____________________

3. 736,120 ____________________

4. 5,824,416 ____________________

5. 9,301,558 ____________________

What's My Number?

WRITE the number.

HINT: Don't forget the comma after the millions place and the thousands place. Starting at the right, count every three digits to the left and add a comma.

1. 6,942 six thousand, nine hundred forty-two
2. ______ five hundred sixty-four thousand, one hundred eighty-one
3. ______ two million, two hundred twenty-three thousand, eight hundred forty-six
4. ______ ninety thousand, three hundred thirty-seven
5. ______ four million, one hundred nineteen thousand, six hundred seventy-three
6. ______ seven thousand, three hundred fourteen
7. ______ one million, eight hundred eighty-two thousand, four hundred fifty
8. ______ seventy-six thousand, five hundred eight
9. ______ two hundred thirty thousand, seven hundred twenty-nine
10. ______ seven million, four hundred ninety-one thousand, two hundred seventy-seven

Find Your Place

IDENTIFY the place of each digit. Then WRITE the digit.

Example:

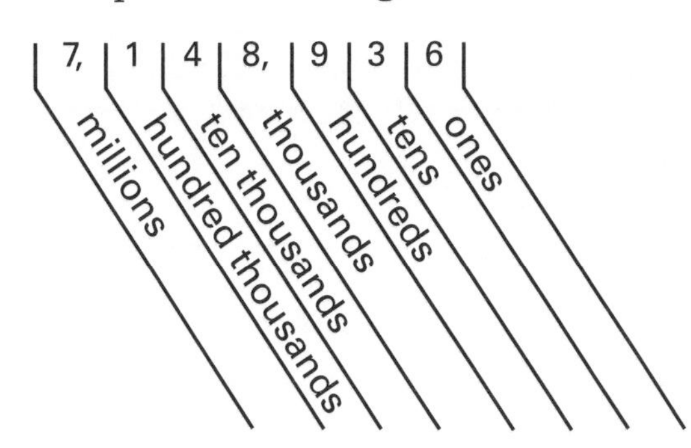

1. 8,523,762

<u>8</u> millions
<u>5</u> hundred thousands
<u>2</u> ten thousands
<u>3</u> thousands
<u>7</u> hundreds
<u>6</u> tens
<u>2</u> ones

2. 1,994,857

____ millions
____ hundred thousands
____ ten thousands
____ thousands
____ hundreds
____ tens
____ ones

3. 4,370,284

____ millions
____ hundred thousands
____ ten thousands
____ thousands
____ hundreds
____ tens
____ ones

4. 6,251,319

____ millions
____ hundred thousands
____ ten thousands
____ thousands
____ hundreds
____ tens
____ ones

5. 7,842,523

____ millions
____ hundred thousands
____ ten thousands
____ thousands
____ hundreds
____ tens
____ ones

6. 5,719,688

____ millions
____ hundred thousands
____ ten thousands
____ thousands
____ hundreds
____ tens
____ ones

High Fives

FIND the 5 in each number. WRITE the place of each 5.

1. 3,533,972 ______hundred thousands______ place
2. 6,085,427 ____________________ place
3. 5,174,819 ____________________ place
4. 2,940,758 ____________________ place
5. 8,258,133 ____________________ place
6. 1,719,605 ____________________ place
7. 3,562,394 ____________________ place
8. 9,894,541 ____________________ place

Mismatched

WRITE > or < in each box.

			#				#
907	>	738	1	612		599	2
776		862	3	423		2,423	4
5,275		891	5	1,006		950	6
6,472		3,565	7	8,717		7,818	8
4,063		4,157	9	9,899		10,099	10
32,751		51,336	11	12,655		12,461	12
103,003		88,724	13	642,195		448,449	14
854,545		548,484	15	365,272		365,709	16

Matched or Mismatched?

WRITE >, <, or = in each box.

	Box			Box	
4,080,867	1	6,959,864	2,777,549	2	1,696,093
5,623,452	3	5,623,452	2,785,975	4	1,536,698
7,928,059	5	9,507,088	6,471,341	6	8,459,450
4,892,580	7	4,892,580	3,470,189	8	3,578,206
1,116,896	9	1,128,553	8,295,416	10	8,290,643
7,580,088	11	7,583,130	5,494,364	12	5,492,964
9,746,931	13	9,746,959	6,016,551	14	6,016,551
2,173,219	15	2,173,419	4,999,016	16	4,999,009

Which One?

CIRCLE the largest number in each row.

1. 5,036 6,874 5,239 6,790

2. 10,175 9,628 11,160 10,181

3. 26,696 25,217 28,879 27,688

4. 680,391 634,805 650,864 678,945

5. 3,085,780 3,162,983 3,112,536 3,186,797

6. 7,194,027 7,198,003 7,006,472 7,156,321

Which One?

CIRCLE the smallest number in each row.

1.	3,420	4,038	3,877	3,975
2.	16,516	14,359	15,078	14,238
3.	45,348	46,070	45,297	45,904
4.	912,531	852,268	902,277	885,648
5.	4,163,588	4,647,766	4,531,690	4,290,312
6.	6,267,832	6,299,421	6,267,828	6,301,005

Round About

Rounding makes numbers easier to work with.

Numbers that end in 1 through 499 get rounded **down** to the nearest thousand.

Numbers that end in 500 through 999 get rounded **up** to the nearest thousand.

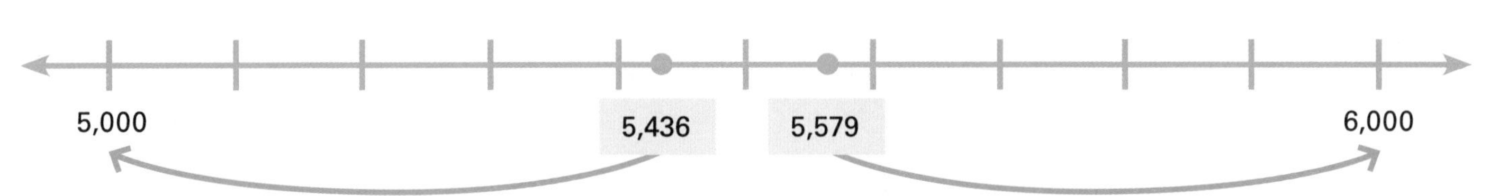

Numbers that end in 1 through 4,999 get rounded **down** to the nearest ten thousand.

Numbers that end in 5,000 through 9,999 get rounded **up** to the nearest ten thousand.

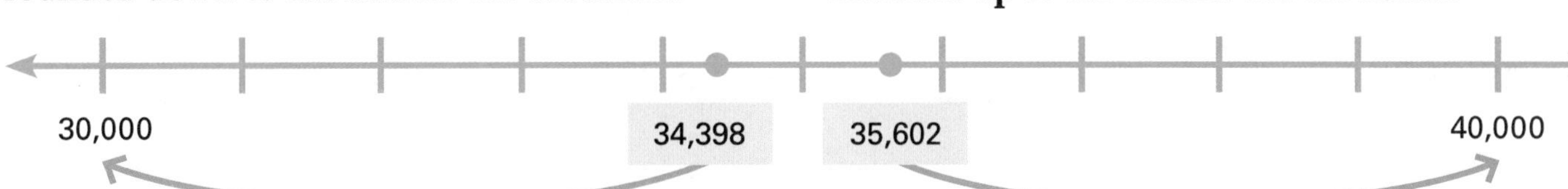

ROUND to the nearest thousand.

1. 1,024 ________
2. 7,885 ________
3. 6,133 ________
4. 8,647 ________
5. 2,712 ________
6. 4,603 ________
7. 9,428 ________
8. 4,530 ________
9. 5,499 ________

ROUND to the nearest ten thousand.

10. 83,723 ________
11. 17,607 ________
12. 23,652 ________
13. 58,149 ________
14. 62,996 ________
15. 74,342 ________
16. 15,890 ________
17. 44,444 ________
18. 33,501 ________

Round About

Numbers that end in 1 through 49,999 get rounded **down** to the nearest hundred thousand. 635,612 → 600,000

Numbers that end in 50,000 through 99,999 get rounded **up** to the nearest hundred thousand. 659,782 → 700,000

Numbers that end in 1 through 499,999 get rounded **down** to the nearest million. 1,422,034 → 1,000,000

Numbers that end in 500,000 through 999,999 get rounded **up** to the nearest million. 1,599,278 → 2,000,000

ROUND to the nearest hundred thousand.

1. 707,269 ____________
2. 595,389 ____________
3. 133,805 ____________
4. 360,056 ____________
5. 225,173 ____________
6. 968,615 ____________
7. 448,883 ____________
8. 556,724 ____________

ROUND to the nearest million.

9. 3,248,955 ____________
10. 9,313,548 ____________
11. 4,701,205 ____________
12. 7,119,125 ____________
13. 5,212,111 ____________
14. 1,492,166 ____________
15. 2,566,089 ____________
16. 6,430,209 ____________

Guess and Check

Estimating is making a reasonable guess about something. How many jellybeans are on this page? WRITE your estimate. Then CIRCLE a group of 20 jellybeans. WRITE a new estimate. CHECK page 119 to see how close your estimates were.

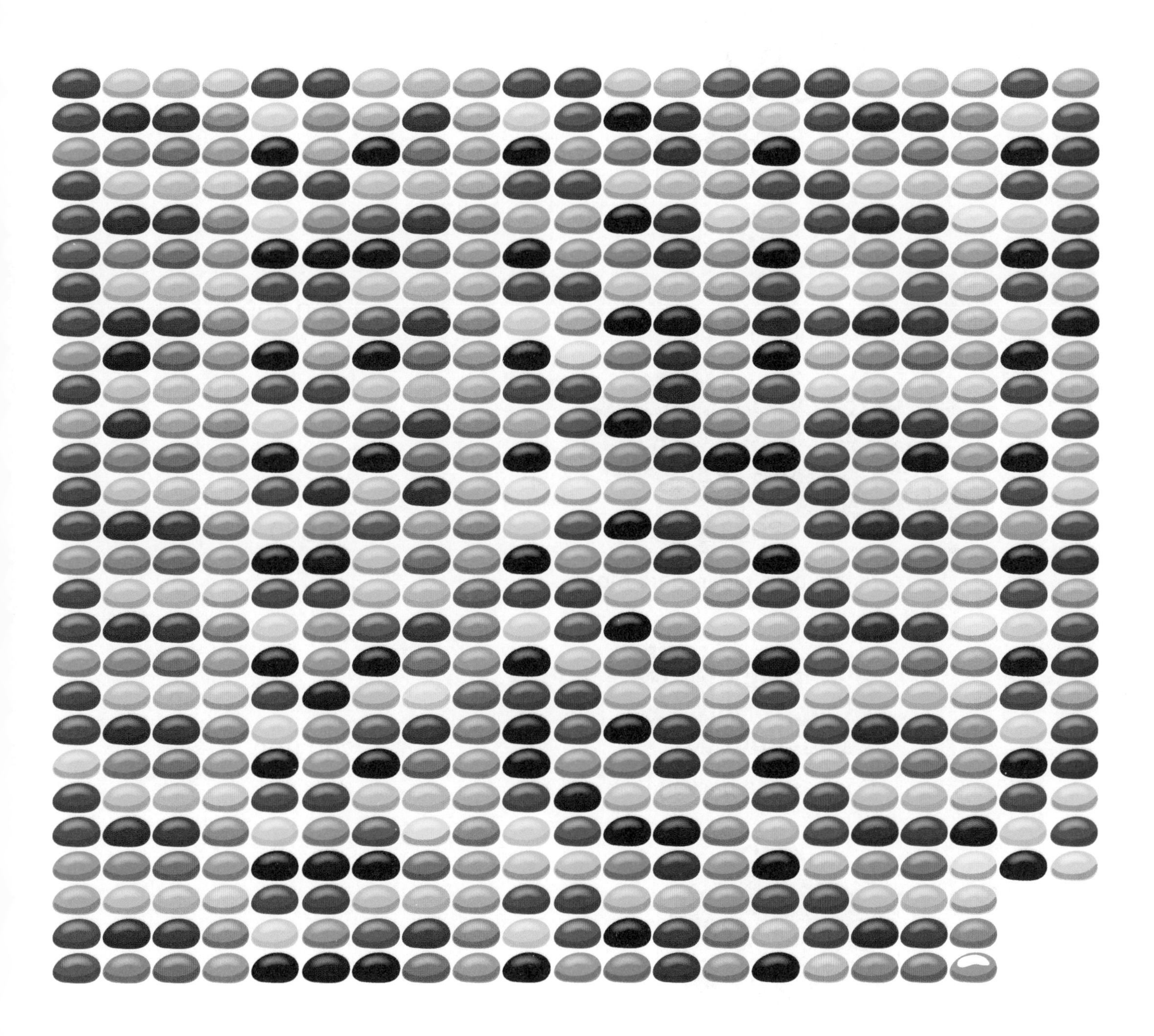

Estimate 1: ______________ Estimate 2: ______________ Check: ______________

Match Up

DRAW a line to match each picture with a reasonable estimate.

Pages in a dictionary

50

Staples in a box

3,000,000

Stars visible on a clear, dark night

1,800

Cookies in a package

200,000

Leaves on a tree

5,000

Unit Rewind

WRITE each number.

1. six hundred eighty-two thousand, four hundred thirteen ____________

2. one hundred sixty-seven thousand, five hundred twenty-one ____________

3. nine million, seventy-six thousand, eight hundred three ____________

WRITE the number words.

4. 34,987 ____

____

5. 458,013 ____

____

6. 5,324,995 ____

____

CIRCLE the number.

7. Which number has a 7 in the hundred thousands place?

1,375,421 3,782,903 7,953,492

8. Which number has a 5 in the millions place?

5,712,436 9,251,084 6,582,317

9. Which number has an 8 in the ten thousands place?

2,038,935 3,860,729 1,989,236

Unit Rewind

WRITE >, <, or = in each box.

3,302,695	1	2,382,127	5,858,624	2	5,095,486
9,649,143	3	9,755,083	1,561,742	4	1,608,438
4,360,801	5	4,360,801	8,183,090	6 	8,182,977

ROUND each number to the nearest thousand, ten thousand, hundred thousand, and million.

	2,391,457	5,926,592	9,465,617
7. Nearest thousand	________	________	________
8. Nearest ten thousand	________	________	________
9. Nearest hundred thousand	________	________	________
10. Nearest million	________	________	________

CIRCLE a reasonable estimate for the number of apples in a bushel.

11. 10   100   1,000   10,000

It All Adds Up

To add large numbers, start with the ones and work left.

Add the ones.	Add the tens.	Add the hundreds.	Add the thousands.	Add the ten thousands.
53,045 + 12,230 5	53,045 + 12,230 75	53,045 + 12,230 275	53,045 + 12,230 5,275	53,045 + 12,230 65,275

WRITE each sum.

1. 84,156 + 3,812

2. 16,314 + 1,142

3. 51,231 + 2,724

4. 20,422 + 9,262

5. 41,602 + 17,113

6. 71,477 + 23,120

7. 16,022 + 10,171

8. 31,163 + 48,101

9. 20,114 + 20,122

10. 32,340 + 52,413

11. 31,231 + 34,411

12. 45,481 + 14,214

Pick Apart

Partial sums is a method of addition, adding each place one at a time.

		42,784
		+ 26,197
Add the numbers in the ten thousands place.	40,000 + 20,000 =	60,000
Add the numbers in the thousands place.	2,000 + 6,000 =	8,000
Add the numbers in the hundreds place.	700 + 100 =	800
Add the numbers in the tens place.	80 + 90 =	170
Add the numbers in the ones place.	4 + 7 =	+ 11
The answer is 60,000 + 8,000 + 800 + 170 + 11.		68,981

WRITE each sum using partial sums.

1. 52,228 + 26,355

2. 31,496 + 33,282

3. 71,024 + 19,936

4. 47,343 + 25,748

5. 11,433 + 35,793

6. 48,733 + 50,896

7. 12,114 + 13,924

8. 53,742 + 35,723

It All Adds Up

Whenever the sum is more than nine, carry the one over to the next place.

1 3 1,8 2 4 + 4 3,9 7 7 1	1 1 3 1,8 2 4 + 4 3,9 7 7 0 1	1 1 1 3 1,8 2 4 + 4 3,9 7 7 8 0 1	1 1 1 3 1,8 2 4 + 4 3,9 7 7 5,8 0 1	1 1 1 3 1,8 2 4 + 4 3,9 7 7 7 5,8 0 1
Add the ones. 4 + 7 = 11	Add the tens. 1 + 2 + 7 = 10	Add the hundreds. 1 + 8 + 9 = 18	Add the thousands. 1 + 1 + 3 = 5	Add the ten thousands. 3 + 4 = 7

WRITE each sum.

1. 47,196 + 2,986

2. 33,589 + 7,820

3. 86,353 + 5,975

4. 71,417 + 4,826

5. 55,537 + 13,484

6. 46,416 + 51,624

7. 16,273 + 16,876

8. 37,232 + 18,099

9. 25,804 + 52,209

10. 42,839 + 46,399

11. 43,375 + 19,707

12. 19,067 + 23,755

It All Adds Up

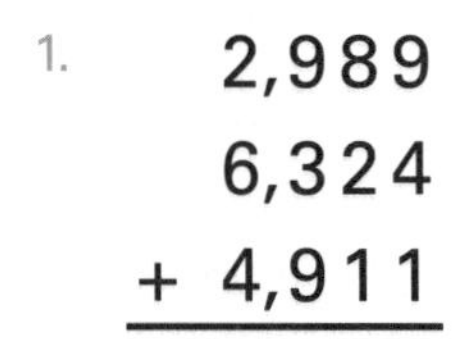

WRITE each sum.

1.
  2,989
  6,324
+ 4,911

2.
  3,076
  8,144
+ 3,885

3.
  7,623
  9,758
+ 2,566

4.
  5,853
  4,610
+ 7,899

5.
  35,118
  2,554
+ 6,307

6.
  48,551
  1,964
+ 5,213

7.
  12,457
  23,794
+ 29,381

8.
  36,680
  42,787
+ 16,632

9.
  19,237
  3,199
  8,513
+ 3,551

10.
  25,864
  52,428
  7,445
+ 1,197

11.
  48,319
  15,523
  22,993
+ 4,701

12.
  10,832
  23,614
  11,513
+ 13,922

What's the Difference?

To subtract large numbers, start with the ones and work left.

Subtract the ones.	Subtract the tens.	Subtract the hundreds.	Subtract the thousands.	Subtract the ten thousands.
74,667 − 23,053 = 4	74,667 − 23,053 = 14	74,667 − 23,053 = 614	74,667 − 23,053 = 1,614	74,667 − 23,053 = 51,614

WRITE each difference.

1. 28,932 − 7,211

2. 54,986 − 1,950

3. 95,459 − 2,026

4. 79,137 − 2,035

5. 88,589 − 75,460

6. 72,527 − 21,314

7. 83,596 − 22,191

8. 65,939 − 22,415

9. 79,438 − 74,110

10. 67,798 − 45,058

11. 26,739 − 12,114

12. 49,681 − 10,330

What's the Difference?

Whenever the digit on top is smaller, regroup numbers from the next place to the left.

5 13 79,163 − 17,459 4	5 13 79,163 − 17,459 04	8 11 5 13 79,163 − 17,459 704	8 11 5 13 79,163 − 17,459 1,704	8 11 5 13 79,163 − 17,459 61,704
Subtract the ones. Regroup 1 from the tens place. 13 − 9 = 4	Subtract the tens. 5 − 5 = 0	Subtract the hundreds. Regroup 1 from the thousands place. 11 − 4 = 7	Subtract the thousands. 8 − 7 = 1	Subtract the ten thousands. 7 − 1 = 6

WRITE each difference.

1. 50,635 − 7,048

2. 11,515 − 3,648

3. 66,723 − 8,851

4. 78,596 − 8,987

5. 46,932 − 21,374

6. 59,652 − 10,867

7. 92,821 − 86,474

8. 82,714 − 33,263

9. 91,894 − 16,759

10. 33,862 − 19,079

11. 54,692 − 24,715

12. 36,002 − 12,820

Trade First

With the **trade-first** method, you do all of the regrouping at once.

67,634 − 21,928	6 16 2 14 6 ~~7~~,~~6~~ ~~3~~ ~~4~~ − 21,928	6 16 2 14 6 ~~7~~,~~6~~ ~~3~~ ~~4~~ − 21,928 45,706
Look for any place where the bottom digit is too large to be subtracted from the top digit.	Do all of the regrouping at once.	Then subtract each place.

WRITE each difference using the trade-first method.

1. 46,256 − 8,931
2. 74,597 − 9,068
3. 31,042 − 2,305
4. 50,510 − 6,954
5. 24,414 − 19,599
6. 91,412 − 33,649
7. 66,135 − 40,697
8. 22,792 − 10,856
9. 99,087 − 13,459
10. 49,516 − 21,686
11. 77,188 − 37,519
12. 40,770 − 27,158

What's the Difference

WRITE each difference.

HINT: Try using the methods of the last two pages, and decide which one works best for you.

1. 41,821 − 4,387

2. 64,253 − 1,746

3. 82,882 − 5,754

4. 96,630 − 7,316

5. 91,705 − 3,028

6. 19,052 − 1,416

7. 24,008 − 9,725

8. 56,041 − 4,550

9. 70,151 − 44,302

10. 53,314 − 20,728

11. 28,526 − 16,549

12. 38,607 − 36,594

13. 65,087 − 24,719

14. 79,662 − 48,845

15. 17,391 − 14,999

16. 81,139 − 73,252

Number Drop-off

Front-end estimation is a fast way to determine approximately how large a sum or difference will be. For front-end estimation, make all but the leftmost digit of each number zero.

81,207 →	80,000	81,207 becomes 80,000.
+ 6,552 →	+ 6,000	6,552 becomes 6,000.
	86,000	80,000 + 6,000 = 86,000
		81,207 + 6,552 = 87,759

ESTIMATE each sum or difference using front-end estimation. Then WRITE the actual sum or difference to see how close your estimate was.

1. 8,576 + 1,259   + ______

2. 9,662 − 2,314   − ______

3. 30,862 + 2,775   + ______

4. 46,237 − 4,669   − ______

5. 40,927 + 35,290   + ______

6. 99,730 − 57,594   − ______

Rounding Estimates

Rounding numbers before adding and subtracting them often produces a closer estimate than using front-end estimation.

68,231	→	70,000	68,231 rounded to the nearest ten thousand is 70,000.
+ 13,175	→	+ 10,000	13,175 rounded to the nearest ten thousand is 10,000.
		80,000	70,000 + 10,000 = 80,000
			68,231 + 13,175 = 81,406

ESTIMATE each sum or difference by rounding to the nearest ten thousand. WRITE the actual sum or difference to see how close your estimate was.

1. 19,343 + 40,489 = ______   + ______

2. 53,677 − 24,156 = ______   − ______

3. 65,563 + 12,498 = ______   + ______

4. 79,432 − 42,722 = ______   − ______

5. 57,249 + 28,501 = ______   + ______

6. 64,205 − 52,198 = ______   − ______

Work It Out

The Cooperstown Comets are playing their first series of the season. On Friday, 38,543 tickets were sold. On Saturday, 35,231 tickets were sold. Sunday was cold and windy and only 17,906 tickets were sold.

1. What was the total number of tickets sold for this series? ________

2. The Comets' Stadium has 42,000 seats. How many seats are empty on a day when 29,674 tickets are sold? ________

Unit Rewind

First, ESTIMATE each problem using front-end estimation. Then ESTIMATE each problem by rounding to the nearest ten thousand. WRITE the sum or difference to compare your estimates.

	Problem	Front End	Rounding
1.	48,369 + 38,848	+ ____	+ ____
2.	20,128 + 12,856	+ ____	+ ____
3.	77,807 − 54,431	− ____	− ____
4.	68,324 − 11,584	− ____	− ____

Pesky Products

A **multiplication table** shows the products you get when you multiply numbers in the first row with the numbers in the first column. WRITE the missing numbers on the multiplication table.

×	0	1	2	3	4	5	6	7	8	9	10
0	0	0	0	0	0		0	0		0	0
1		1	2		4	5		7	8		10
2	0		4	6		10	12		16	18	
3	0	3		9	12		18	21		27	30
4		4	8		16	20		28	32		40
5	0		10	15		25	30		40	45	
6	0	6		18	24		36	42		54	60
7		7	14		28	35		49	56		70
8	0		16	24		40	48		64	72	
9	0	9		27	36		54	63		81	90
10		10	20		40	50		70	80		100

Computation Station

A **product** is the number you get when you multiply two numbers. WRITE each product.

1. $5 \times 3 =$ ____
2. $8 \times 9 =$ ____
3. $6 \times 1 =$ ____
4. $2 \times 7 =$ ____
5. $3 \times 10 =$ ____
6. $6 \times 6 =$ ____
7. $8 \times 7 =$ ____
8. $5 \times 0 =$ ____
9. $8 \times 8 =$ ____
10. $5 \times 2 =$ ____
11. $7 \times 9 =$ ____
12. $10 \times 10 =$ ____

13. 6×5
14. 1×3
15. 7×6
16. 9×4
17. 10×8
18. 5×5

19. 9×3
20. 0×1
21. 5×2
22. 9×9
23. 6×4
24. 9×2

25. 7×7
26. 10×2
27. 3×3
28. 7×1
29. 8×6
30. 4×4

Picture It

When multiplying a two-digit number, think of it as tens and ones.

Example: 67 × 5 = 335

6 tens and 7 ones

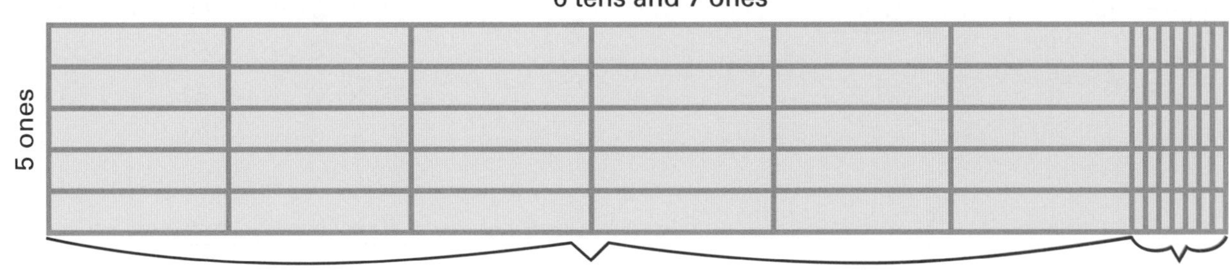

6 tens × 5 ones = 30 tens, or 300

7 ones × 5 ones = 35 ones, or 35

300 + 35 = 335

67 × 5 = 335

Use the pictures to help you answer the problems. WRITE each product.

1. 53 × 8 = ______

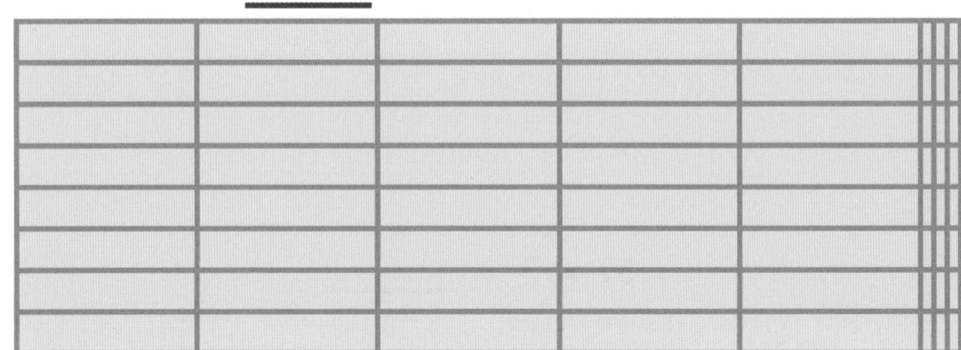

2. 39 × 4 = ______

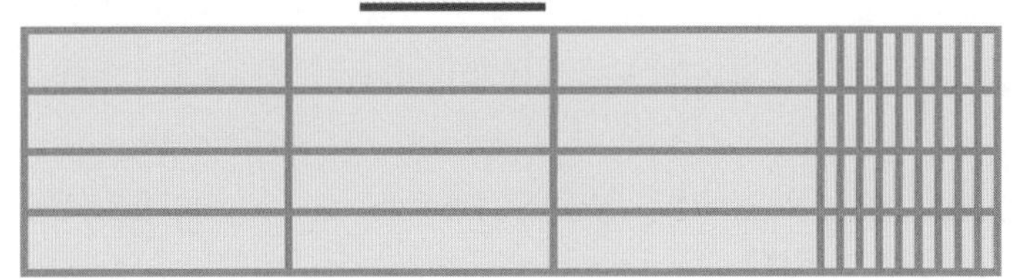

3. 48 × 7 = ______

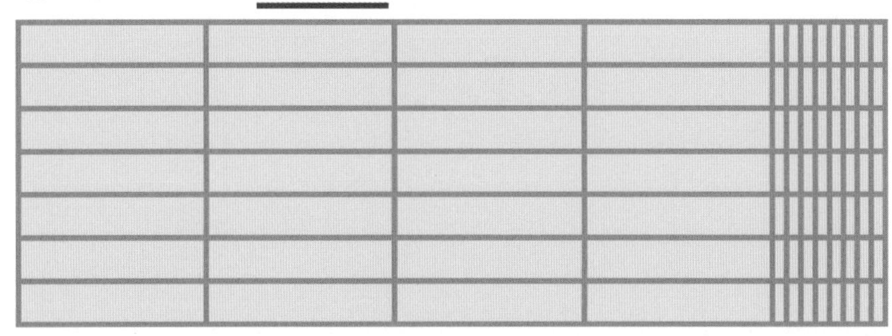

Break It Down

Break down each problem into simple multiplication problems whose products can be added together. WRITE each product.

Example: 54 × 6 = 324

54 = 10 + 10 + 10 + 10 + 10 + 4

10 × 6 = 60
10 × 6 = 60
10 × 6 = 60
10 × 6 = 60
10 × 6 = 60
4 × 6 = + 24
324

1. 18 × 9 = ______

2. 46 × 5 = ______

3. 62 × 7 = ______

4. 57 × 3 = ______

5. 23 × 4 = ______

6. 35 × 8 = ______

Computation Station

WRITE each product.

Example:

72 × 4 = 8	72 × 4 = 288
Multiply the ones. 2 × 4 = 8 ones	Multiply the tens. 7 × 4 = 28 tens, or 280

1. 24 × 2
2. 79 × 1
3. 31 × 9
4. 44 × 2
5. 13 × 3
6. 62 × 4
7. 84 × 2
8. 93 × 2
9. 50 × 8
10. 64 × 2
11. 73 × 3
12. 20 × 7
13. 91 × 6
14. 63 × 2
15. 87 × 1
16. 40 × 9
17. 52 × 4
18. 71 × 5

Computation Station

WRITE each product.

Example:

$\begin{array}{r} {}^{3} \\ 65 \\ \times\ 7 \\ \hline 5 \end{array}$	$\begin{array}{r} {}^{3} \\ 65 \\ \times\ 7 \\ \hline 455 \end{array}$
Multiply the ones. 5 × 7 = 35 ones Write 5 in the ones place and carry 3 tens.	Multiply the tens. 6 × 7 = 42 tens + 3 tens = 45 tens, or 450

1. $\begin{array}{r} 57 \\ \times\ 2 \\ \hline \end{array}$
2. $\begin{array}{r} 96 \\ \times\ 3 \\ \hline \end{array}$
3. $\begin{array}{r} 72 \\ \times\ 9 \\ \hline \end{array}$
4. $\begin{array}{r} 35 \\ \times\ 6 \\ \hline \end{array}$
5. $\begin{array}{r} 88 \\ \times\ 4 \\ \hline \end{array}$
6. $\begin{array}{r} 43 \\ \times\ 7 \\ \hline \end{array}$
7. $\begin{array}{r} 26 \\ \times\ 8 \\ \hline \end{array}$
8. $\begin{array}{r} 65 \\ \times\ 5 \\ \hline \end{array}$
9. $\begin{array}{r} 33 \\ \times\ 8 \\ \hline \end{array}$
10. $\begin{array}{r} 16 \\ \times\ 3 \\ \hline \end{array}$
11. $\begin{array}{r} 47 \\ \times\ 7 \\ \hline \end{array}$
12. $\begin{array}{r} 74 \\ \times\ 4 \\ \hline \end{array}$
13. $\begin{array}{r} 34 \\ \times\ 9 \\ \hline \end{array}$
14. $\begin{array}{r} 76 \\ \times\ 8 \\ \hline \end{array}$
15. $\begin{array}{r} 19 \\ \times\ 6 \\ \hline \end{array}$
16. $\begin{array}{r} 53 \\ \times\ 4 \\ \hline \end{array}$
17. $\begin{array}{r} 99 \\ \times\ 7 \\ \hline \end{array}$
18. $\begin{array}{r} 85 \\ \times\ 9 \\ \hline \end{array}$

Computation Station

WRITE each product.

Example:

$\begin{array}{r} {}^{5}\\ 149 \\ \times \quad 6 \\ \hline 4 \end{array}$	$\begin{array}{r} {}^{2\,5}\\ 149 \\ \times \quad 6 \\ \hline 94 \end{array}$	$\begin{array}{r} {}^{2\,5}\\ 149 \\ \times \quad 6 \\ \hline 894 \end{array}$
Multiply the ones. 9 x 6 = 54 ones Write 4 in the ones place and carry 5 tens.	Multiply the tens. 4 x 6 = 24 tens + 5 tens = 29 tens, or 290 Write 9 in the tens place and carry 2 hundreds.	Multiply the hundreds. 1 x 6 = 6 hundreds + 2 hundreds = 8 hundreds, or 800.

1. $\begin{array}{r} 352 \\ \times \quad 2 \\ \hline \end{array}$
2. $\begin{array}{r} 438 \\ \times \quad 4 \\ \hline \end{array}$
3. $\begin{array}{r} 816 \\ \times \quad 9 \\ \hline \end{array}$
4. $\begin{array}{r} 142 \\ \times \quad 6 \\ \hline \end{array}$
5. $\begin{array}{r} 767 \\ \times \quad 5 \\ \hline \end{array}$
6. $\begin{array}{r} 295 \\ \times \quad 7 \\ \hline \end{array}$
7. $\begin{array}{r} 807 \\ \times \quad 3 \\ \hline \end{array}$
8. $\begin{array}{r} 182 \\ \times \quad 5 \\ \hline \end{array}$
9. $\begin{array}{r} 332 \\ \times \quad 4 \\ \hline \end{array}$
10. $\begin{array}{r} 675 \\ \times \quad 1 \\ \hline \end{array}$
11. $\begin{array}{r} 514 \\ \times \quad 7 \\ \hline \end{array}$
12. $\begin{array}{r} 270 \\ \times \quad 9 \\ \hline \end{array}$
13. $\begin{array}{r} 454 \\ \times \quad 6 \\ \hline \end{array}$
14. $\begin{array}{r} 563 \\ \times \quad 2 \\ \hline \end{array}$
15. $\begin{array}{r} 319 \\ \times \quad 8 \\ \hline \end{array}$
16. $\begin{array}{r} 272 \\ \times \quad 5 \\ \hline \end{array}$
17. $\begin{array}{r} 928 \\ \times \quad 3 \\ \hline \end{array}$
18. $\begin{array}{r} 198 \\ \times \quad 9 \\ \hline \end{array}$

Pick Apart

Partial products is a method of multiplication, multiplying each place one at a time.

		682
		× 7
Multiply the hundreds.	600 × 7 =	4,200
Multiply the tens.	80 × 7 =	560
Multiply the ones.	2 × 7 =	+ 14
Then add the numbers together.		4,774

WRITE each product using partial products.

1. 455 × 8
2. 372 × 2
3. 518 × 4
4. 796 × 5
5. 189 × 6
6. 231 × 8
7. 574 × 7
8. 387 × 3
9. 922 × 9
10. 437 × 5

Computation Station

When you multiply by a two-digit number, multiply one place at a time.

$\begin{array}{r} {}^{1\,3}\\ 427 \\ \times\ 35 \\ \hline 2,135 \end{array}$	$\begin{array}{r} {}^{2}\\ 427 \\ \times\ 35 \\ \hline 2,135 \\ 10 \end{array}$	$\begin{array}{r} {}^{2}\\ 427 \\ \times\ 35 \\ \hline 2,135 \\ 810 \end{array}$	$\begin{array}{r} {}^{2}\\ 427 \\ \times\ 35 \\ \hline 2,135 \\ 12,810 \end{array}$	$\begin{array}{r} 427 \\ \times\ 35 \\ \hline 2,135 \\ +\,12,810 \\ \hline 14,945 \end{array}$
Multiply 427 by 5 ones.	Multiply 427 by 3 tens, starting with the ones place. 7 ones × 3 tens = 21 tens, or 210.	Next, multiply the tens place. 2 tens × 3 tens = 6 hundreds + 2 hundreds = 8 hundreds, or 800.	Next, multiply the hundreds place. 4 hundreds × 3 tens = 12 thousands.	Then add 2,135 and 12,810.

WRITE each product.

1. $\begin{array}{r} 54 \\ \times\ 21 \\ \hline \end{array}$
2. $\begin{array}{r} 36 \\ \times\ 15 \\ \hline \end{array}$
3. $\begin{array}{r} 63 \\ \times\ 45 \\ \hline \end{array}$
4. $\begin{array}{r} 74 \\ \times\ 30 \\ \hline \end{array}$
5. $\begin{array}{r} 49 \\ \times\ 72 \\ \hline \end{array}$
6. $\begin{array}{r} 88 \\ \times\ 56 \\ \hline \end{array}$
7. $\begin{array}{r} 90 \\ \times\ 47 \\ \hline \end{array}$
8. $\begin{array}{r} 25 \\ \times\ 25 \\ \hline \end{array}$
9. $\begin{array}{r} 77 \\ \times\ 13 \\ \hline \end{array}$
10. $\begin{array}{r} 93 \\ \times\ 68 \\ \hline \end{array}$
11. $\begin{array}{r} 41 \\ \times\ 19 \\ \hline \end{array}$
12. $\begin{array}{r} 64 \\ \times\ 42 \\ \hline \end{array}$
13. $\begin{array}{r} 731 \\ \times\ 12 \\ \hline \end{array}$
14. $\begin{array}{r} 542 \\ \times\ 34 \\ \hline \end{array}$
15. $\begin{array}{r} 840 \\ \times\ 65 \\ \hline \end{array}$
16. $\begin{array}{r} 267 \\ \times\ 56 \\ \hline \end{array}$
17. $\begin{array}{r} 395 \\ \times\ 27 \\ \hline \end{array}$
18. $\begin{array}{r} 971 \\ \times\ 82 \\ \hline \end{array}$

Pick Apart

Using partial products to multiply by a two-digit number works the same way as with a one-digit number.

Example:

					354
					× 62
Multiply the hundreds.	300	×	60	=	18,000
	300	×	2	=	600
Multiply the tens.	50	×	60	=	3,000
	50	×	2	=	100
Multiply the ones.	4	×	60	=	240
	4	×	2	=	+ 8
Then add the numbers together.					21,948

WRITE each product using partial products.

1. $\begin{array}{r} 34 \\ \times\ 26 \\ \hline \end{array}$

2. $\begin{array}{r} 75 \\ \times\ 42 \\ \hline \end{array}$

3. $\begin{array}{r} 51 \\ \times\ 37 \\ \hline \end{array}$

4. $\begin{array}{r} 92 \\ \times\ 48 \\ \hline \end{array}$

5. $\begin{array}{r} 68 \\ \times\ 16 \\ \hline \end{array}$

6. $\begin{array}{r} 164 \\ \times\ 35 \\ \hline \end{array}$

7. $\begin{array}{r} 379 \\ \times\ 11 \\ \hline \end{array}$

8. $\begin{array}{r} 215 \\ \times\ 59 \\ \hline \end{array}$

9. $\begin{array}{r} 641 \\ \times\ 76 \\ \hline \end{array}$

10. $\begin{array}{r} 827 \\ \times\ 63 \\ \hline \end{array}$

Divide and Conquer

WRITE the missing numbers on each chart.

HINT: Divide the numbers in the top row by the number on the side.

÷	25	5	35	20	50	15	10	30	45	40
5	5									

÷	15	27	12	3	30	18	6	24	9	21
3										

÷	8	48	80	40	16	24	56	72	32	64
8										

÷	24	40	16	20	32	8	12	28	36	4
4										

÷	21	63	28	56	35	70	14	7	49	42
7										

÷	18	90	9	54	63	27	36	72	81	45
9										

Computation Station

A **quotient** is the number you get when you divide one number by another number.
WRITE each quotient.

1. $14 \div 7 =$ ____
2. $63 \div 9 =$ ____
3. $80 \div 8 =$ ____
4. $36 \div 4 =$ ____
5. $72 \div 8 =$ ____
6. $35 \div 5 =$ ____
7. $48 \div 6 =$ ____
8. $16 \div 2 =$ ____
9. $27 \div 3 =$ ____
10. $10 \div 10 =$ ____
11. $21 \div 7 =$ ____
12. $8 \div 1 =$ ____

13. $5\overline{)45}$
14. $9\overline{)90}$
15. $6\overline{)30}$
16. $9\overline{)81}$
17. $3\overline{)15}$

18. $6\overline{)12}$
19. $7\overline{)49}$
20. $10\overline{)100}$
21. $8\overline{)64}$
22. $5\overline{)20}$

23. $7\overline{)7}$
24. $9\overline{)27}$
25. $3\overline{)12}$
26. $7\overline{)70}$
27. $4\overline{)16}$

28. $9\overline{)45}$
29. $1\overline{)5}$
30. $4\overline{)32}$
31. $9\overline{)72}$
32. $7\overline{)63}$

Picture It

Use the pictures to help you find the quotients. WRITE each quotient.

HINT: Imagine you are sharing the shaded blocks with the number of people in the divisor (the number being used to divide).

Example: 60 ÷ 5 = 12

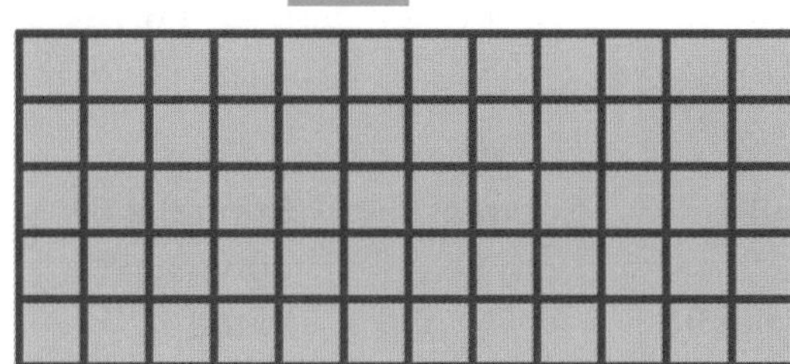

5 rows of 12

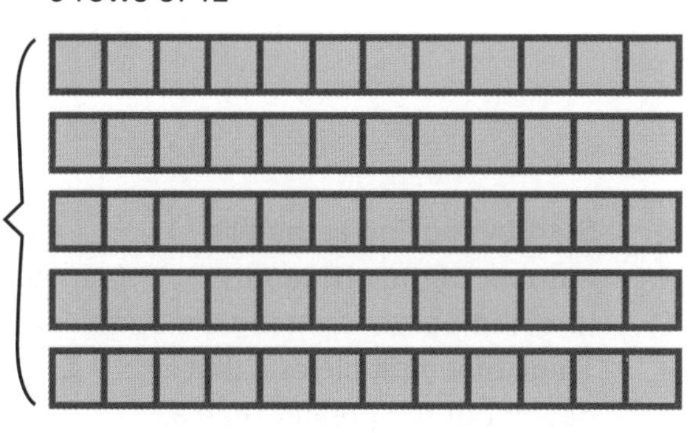

1. 88 ÷ 8 = ____

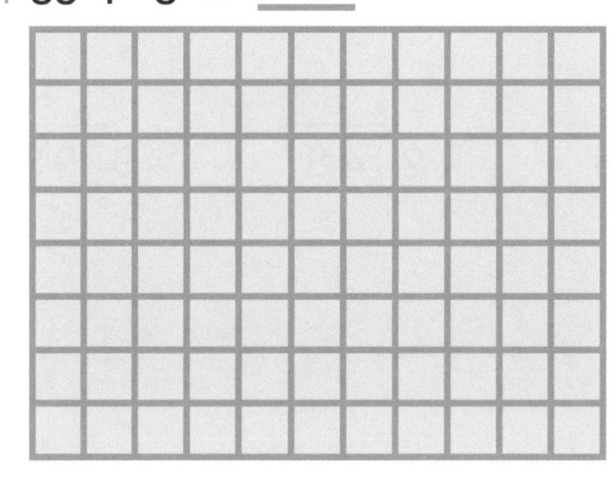

2. 72 ÷ 6 = ____

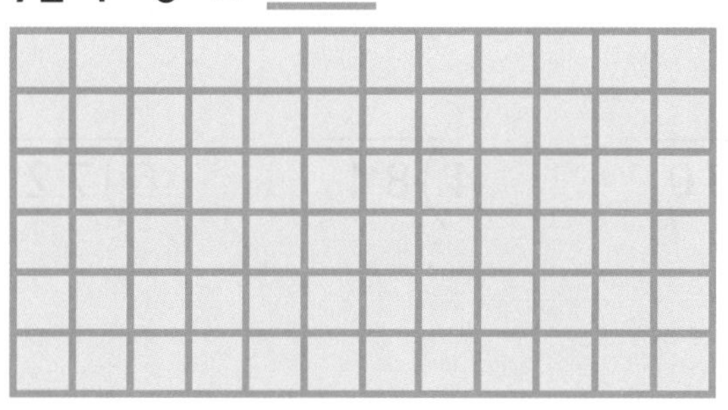

3. 32 ÷ 2 = ____

4. 44 ÷ 11 = ____

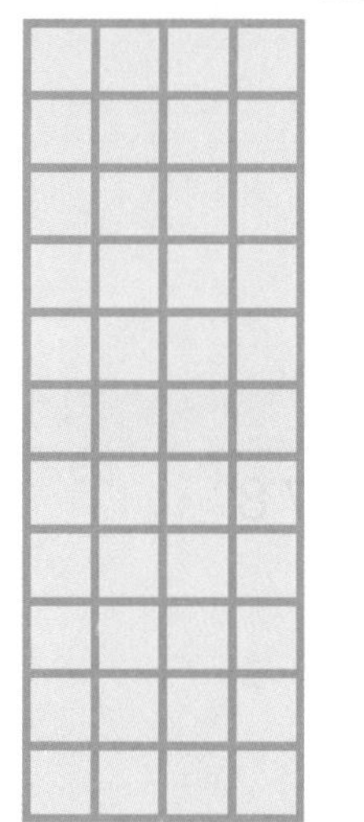

5. 56 ÷ 4 = ____

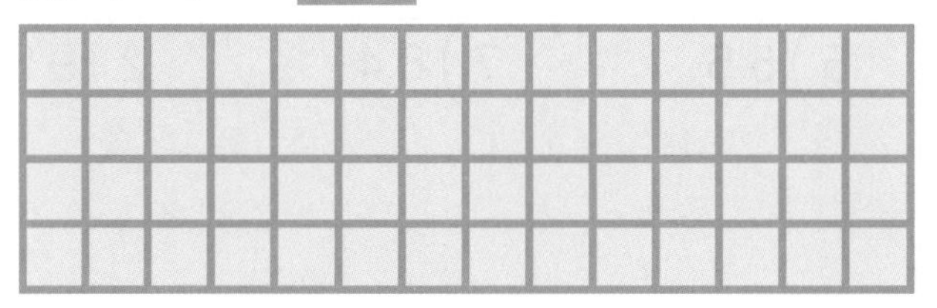

Computation Station

DIVIDE two-digit numbers.

Example:

$4\overline{)96}$	$\begin{array}{r} 2 \\ 4\overline{)96} \\ 8 \end{array}$	$\begin{array}{r} 2 \\ 4\overline{)96} \\ \underline{-8} \\ 1 \end{array}$	$\begin{array}{r} 2 \\ 4\overline{)96} \\ \underline{-8} \\ 16 \end{array}$	$\begin{array}{r} 24 \\ 4\overline{)96} \\ \underline{-8} \\ 16 \\ \underline{-16} \\ 0 \end{array}$
Start by looking at the first number of the dividend (the number that's being divided). Think of a multiple of 4 that is near 9 but not greater than 9.	$4 \times 2 = 8$ Write 2 above the 9 and 8 below it.	Subtract 8 from 9.	Bring the 6 down next to the 1. Now find $16 \div 4$.	$4 \times 4 = 16$ Write 4 in the ones place.

WRITE each quotient.

1. $5\overline{)90}$
2. $4\overline{)84}$
3. $6\overline{)72}$
4. $3\overline{)63}$
5. $2\overline{)48}$
6. $9\overline{)99}$
7. $7\overline{)91}$
8. $2\overline{)92}$
9. $5\overline{)85}$
10. $3\overline{)96}$
11. $2\overline{)50}$
12. $3\overline{)81}$
13. $2\overline{)68}$
14. $6\overline{)78}$
15. $8\overline{)96}$
16. $5\overline{)55}$
17. $7\overline{)84}$
18. $2\overline{)98}$

Computation Station

DIVIDE three-digit numbers.

Example:

$6\overline{)354}$	$\begin{array}{r} 5 \\ 6\overline{)354} \\ 30 \end{array}$	$\begin{array}{r} 5 \\ 6\overline{)354} \\ -30 \\ \hline 5 \end{array}$	$\begin{array}{r} 5 \\ 6\overline{)354} \\ -30 \\ \hline 54 \end{array}$	$\begin{array}{r} 59 \\ 6\overline{)354} \\ -30 \\ \hline 54 \\ -54 \\ \hline 0 \end{array}$
3 cannot be divided by 6, so look to the next digit. Think of a multiple of 6 that is near 35 but not greater than 35.	6 x 5 = 30	Subtract 30 from 35.	Bring the 4 down next to the 5. Now divide 54 by 6.	6 x 9 = 54 Write 9 in the ones place.

WRITE each quotient.

1. $6\overline{)174}$
2. $8\overline{)416}$
3. $5\overline{)310}$
4. $3\overline{)297}$
5. $7\overline{)238}$
6. $2\overline{)126}$
7. $9\overline{)315}$
8. $7\overline{)287}$
9. $5\overline{)415}$
10. $2\overline{)192}$
11. $7\overline{)567}$
12. $8\overline{)640}$
13. $4\overline{)312}$
14. $9\overline{)513}$
15. $3\overline{)372}$

Fact Finder

WRITE the quotient. Then WRITE two division problems and two multiplication problems for the three numbers.

Example:

```
    173
5 ) 865
   -5
    36
   -35
     15
    -15
      0
```

865 ÷ 5 = 173
865 ÷ 173 = 5
5 × 173 = 865
173 × 5 = 865

1. $6\overline{)84}$

___ ÷ ___ = ___
___ ÷ ___ = ___
___ × ___ = ___
___ × ___ = ___

2. $2\overline{)56}$

___ ÷ ___ = ___
___ ÷ ___ = ___
___ × ___ = ___
___ × ___ = ___

3. $9\overline{)594}$

___ ÷ ___ = ___
___ ÷ ___ = ___
___ × ___ = ___
___ × ___ = ___

4. $7\overline{)413}$

___ ÷ ___ = ___
___ ÷ ___ = ___
___ × ___ = ___
___ × ___ = ___

5. $4\overline{)748}$

___ ÷ ___ = ___
___ ÷ ___ = ___
___ × ___ = ___
___ × ___ = ___

6. $3\overline{)816}$

___ ÷ ___ = ___
___ ÷ ___ = ___
___ × ___ = ___
___ × ___ = ___

Computation Station

DIVIDE by a two-digit number.

HINT: Try writing multiples of the divisor before you begin.

Example:

Step 1	Step 2	Step 3	Step 4	Step 5
$12\overline{)552}$	$\begin{array}{r} 4 \\ 12\overline{)552} \\ 48 \end{array}$	$\begin{array}{r} 4 \\ 12\overline{)552} \\ -48 \\ \hline 7 \end{array}$	$\begin{array}{r} 4 \\ 12\overline{)552} \\ -48 \\ \hline 72 \end{array}$	$\begin{array}{r} 46 \\ 12\overline{)552} \\ -48 \\ \hline 72 \\ -72 \\ \hline 0 \end{array}$

WRITE each quotient.

1. $18\overline{)54}$
2. $14\overline{)42}$
3. $11\overline{)55}$
4. $15\overline{)90}$
5. $12\overline{)84}$
6. $16\overline{)192}$
7. $24\overline{)480}$
8. $37\overline{)592}$
9. $17\overline{)663}$
10. $25\overline{)375}$
11. $30\overline{)930}$
12. $68\overline{)884}$
13. $14\overline{)728}$
14. $24\overline{)504}$
15. $38\overline{)950}$

Computation Station

WRITE each quotient. Then MULTIPLY to check your work.

Example:

$$\begin{array}{r} 18 \\ 41\overline{)738} \\ -41 \\ \hline 328 \\ -328 \\ \hline 0 \end{array} \longrightarrow \begin{array}{r} 18 \\ \times 41 \\ \hline 18 \\ +720 \\ \hline 738 \end{array}$$

1. $22\overline{)616}$ → $\times\ 22$

2. $64\overline{)704}$ → $\times\ 64$

3. $12\overline{)432}$ → $\times\ 12$

4. $30\overline{)630}$ → $\times\ 30$

5. $34\overline{)510}$ → $\times\ 34$

6. $14\overline{)728}$ → $\times\ 14$

Work It Out

Ella does 75 jumping jacks, 12 push-ups, and 30 sit-ups every day.

1. What is the total number of exercises that she does in 7 days?

_________ jumping jacks

_________ push-ups

_________ sit-ups

The state is holding its annual hog-calling contest. Each of the 93 counties can send 12 contestants.

2. If each county sends all 12 contestants, what will be the total number of contestants?

_________ contestants

Computation Station

WRITE each product.

1. 34×2
2. 51×3
3. 65×5
4. 18×8
5. 82×4
6. 47×6
7. 853×1
8. 512×9
9. 298×3
10. 405×7
11. 782×5
12. 945×8
13. 83×12
14. 40×37
15. 56×61
16. 99×42
17. 73×27
18. 18×39
19. 322×48
20. 136×90
21. 539×63
22. 414×84
23. 926×32
24. 735×76

Work It Out

Max is playing games at the fair when he discovers he could win a TV with 540 prize tickets. He wants to play only one of the games to win the tickets.

1. How many times would he have to win each game to get to 540 tickets?

   Balloon Pop: 3 tickets ________

   Skee-ball: 5 tickets ________

   Hole in One: 15 tickets ________

Suzie's sticker collection has grown to 832 stickers. She just bought a new 16-page sticker album to hold her stickers.

2. If she puts the same number of stickers on each page, what is the number of stickers that would be on one page?

   ________ stickers

Computation Station

WRITE each quotient.

1. $6\overline{)90}$

2. $3\overline{)84}$

3. $4\overline{)44}$

4. $12\overline{)72}$

5. $16\overline{)80}$

6. $6\overline{)228}$

7. $5\overline{)495}$

8. $3\overline{)381}$

9. $11\overline{)715}$

10. $14\overline{)308}$

WRITE the four different multiplication and division problems for each set of numbers.

11. **4, 5, 20**

___ ÷ ___ = ___

___ ÷ ___ = ___

___ × ___ = ___

___ × ___ = ___

12. **6, 13, 78**

___ ÷ ___ = ___

___ ÷ ___ = ___

___ × ___ = ___

___ × ___ = ___

13. **23, 32, 736**

___ ÷ ___ = ___

___ ÷ ___ = ___

___ × ___ = ___

___ × ___ = ___

Any Way You Slice It

WRITE the fraction for each picture.

Example:

3 ← The **numerator** represents the number of shaded sections.

5 ← The **denominator** represents the total number of sections.

1. —

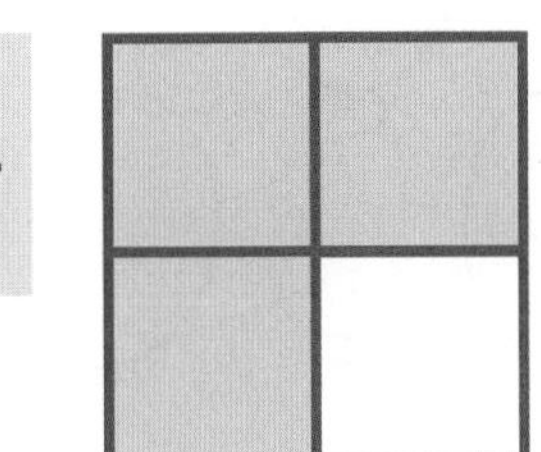

2. —

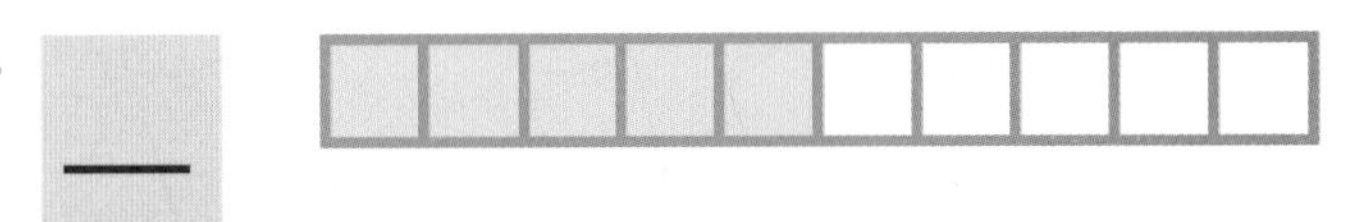

3. —

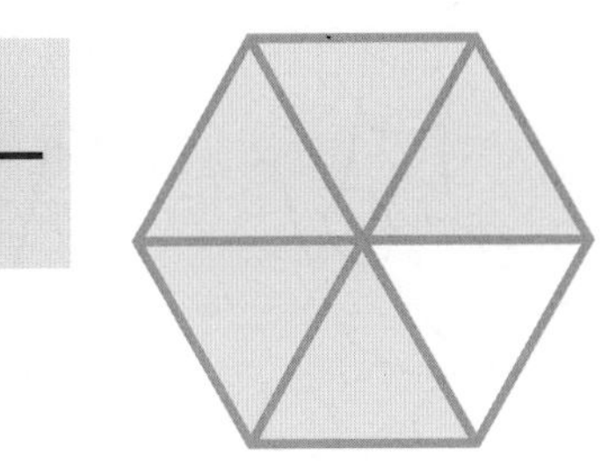

4. —

5. —

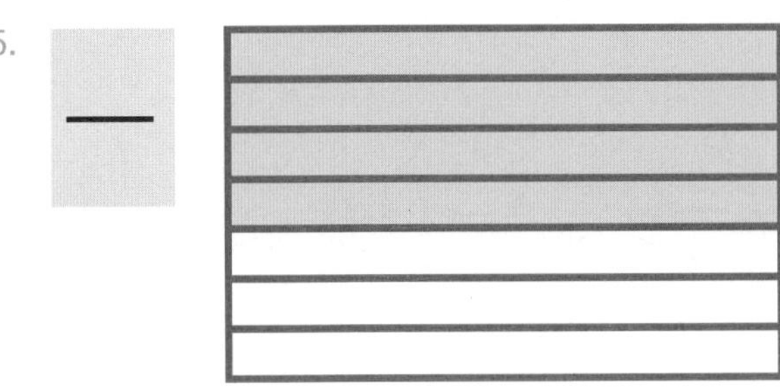

6. —

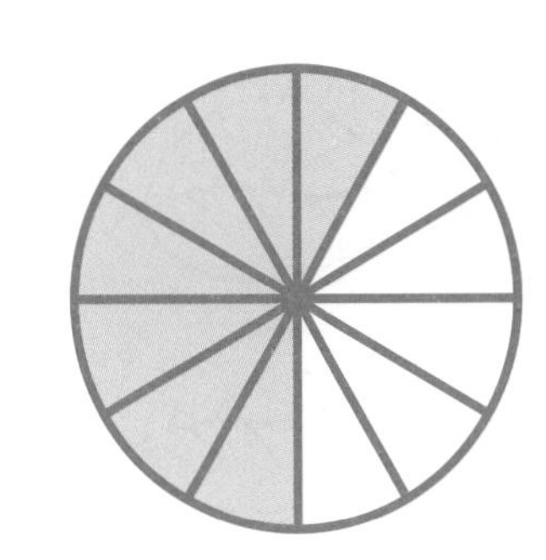

Color Sets

COLOR each set of pictures to match the fraction.

Example:

$\frac{4}{7}$ ← The **numerator** represents the number of colored objects.
← The **denominator** represents the total number of objects.

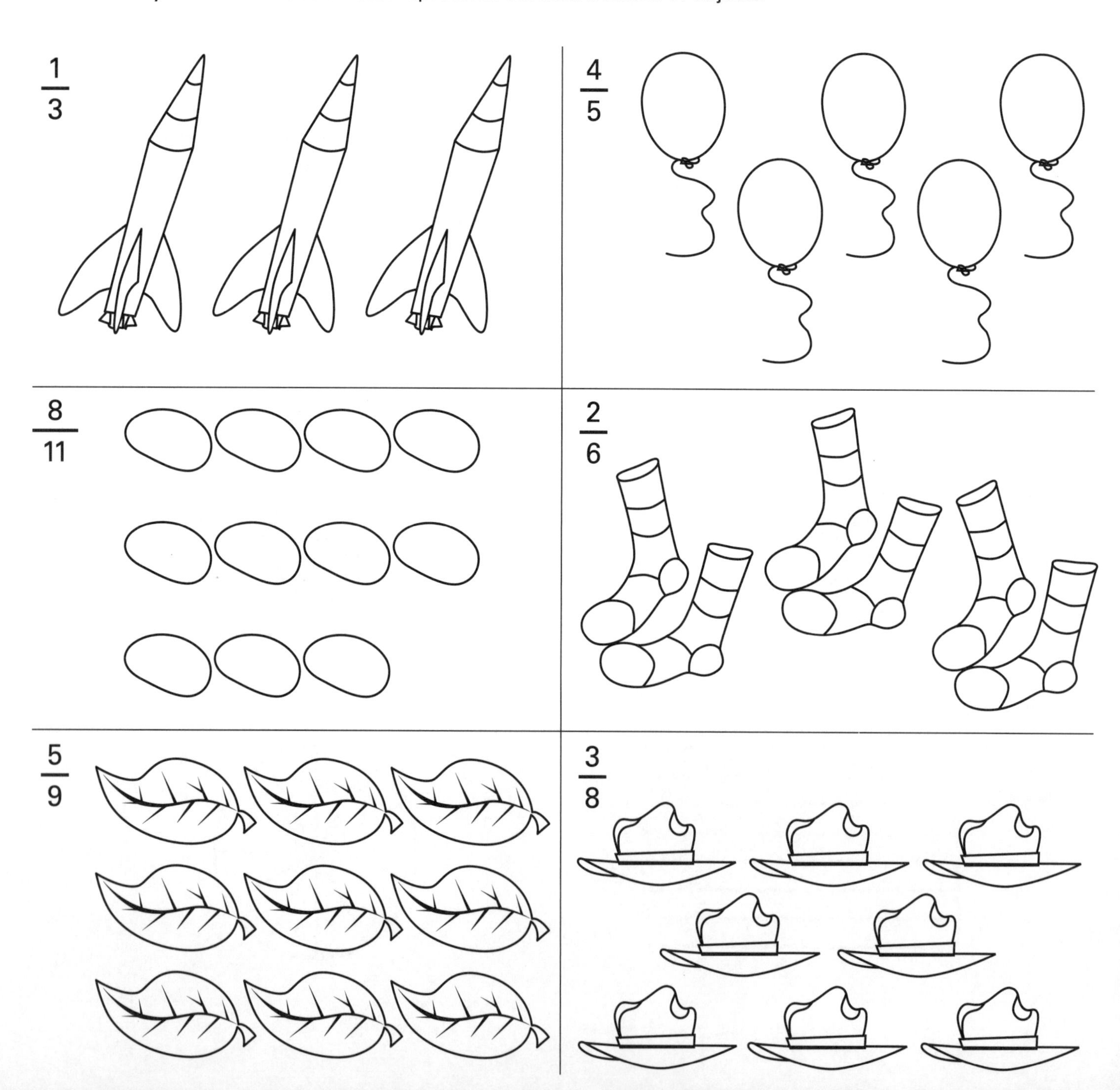

Color and Compare

COLOR the picture to match each fraction. Then CIRCLE the larger fraction.

$\frac{3}{4}$

$\frac{2}{5}$

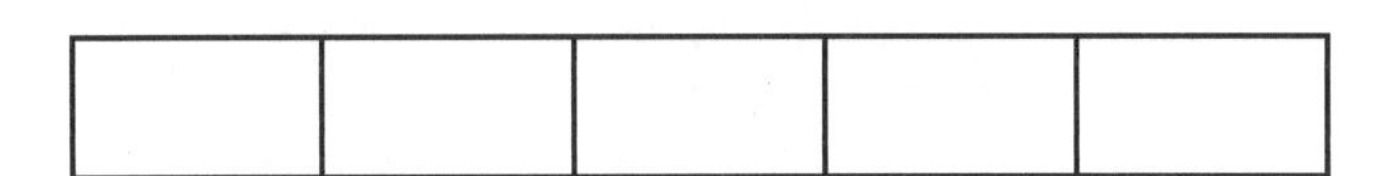

$\frac{1}{6}$

$\frac{1}{3}$

$\frac{2}{3}$

$\frac{4}{8}$

$\frac{5}{6}$

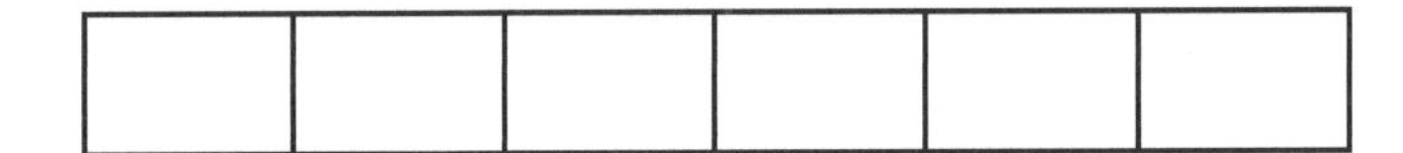

$\frac{6}{7}$

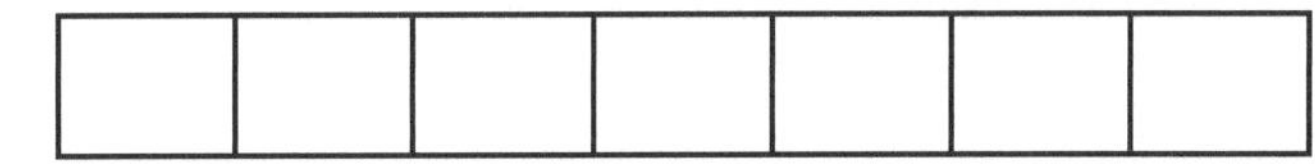

$\frac{7}{12}$

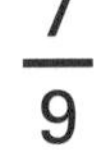

$\frac{7}{9}$

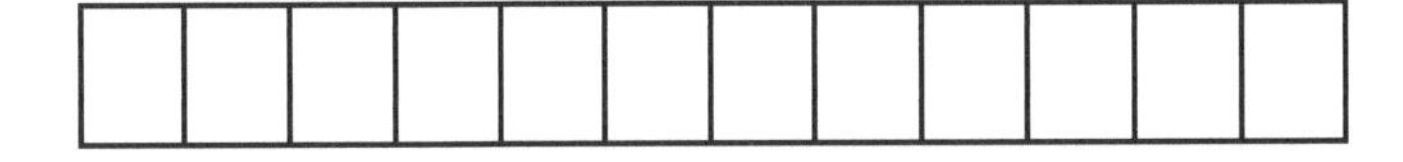

Matched or Mismatched?

WRITE >, <, or = in each box.

HINT: Fractions with larger denominators have smaller individual parts.

Example:

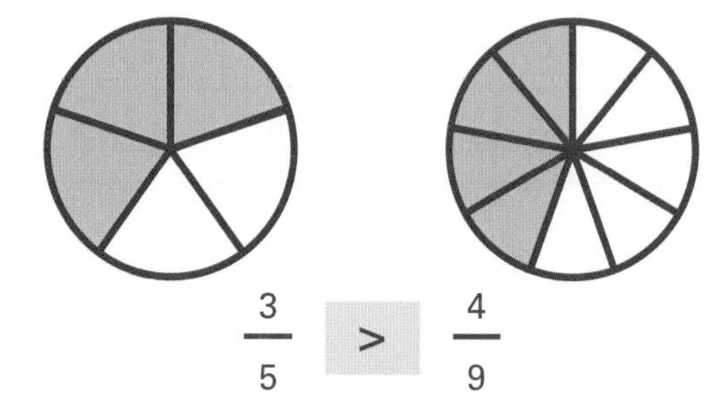

$\frac{3}{5}$ > $\frac{4}{9}$

1. $\frac{3}{4}$ ☐ $\frac{2}{4}$	2. $\frac{1}{7}$ ☐ $\frac{7}{9}$	3. $\frac{3}{12}$ ☐ $\frac{5}{8}$	4. $\frac{2}{5}$ ☐ $\frac{1}{5}$
5. $\frac{6}{10}$ ☐ $\frac{3}{10}$	6. $\frac{1}{2}$ ☐ $\frac{4}{8}$	7. $\frac{6}{6}$ ☐ $\frac{6}{9}$	8. $\frac{3}{7}$ ☐ $\frac{8}{8}$
9. $\frac{1}{3}$ ☐ $\frac{1}{4}$	10. $\frac{4}{6}$ ☐ $\frac{11}{12}$	11. $\frac{2}{9}$ ☐ $\frac{4}{5}$	12. $\frac{4}{9}$ ☐ $\frac{3}{11}$
13. $\frac{3}{4}$ ☐ $\frac{3}{5}$	14. $\frac{7}{11}$ ☐ $\frac{7}{10}$	15. $\frac{6}{6}$ ☐ $\frac{3}{3}$	16. $\frac{5}{2}$ ☐ $\frac{2}{5}$

Fraction Circles

When fractions have the same denominator, add them by adding the numerators only. The denominator stays the same.

Example:

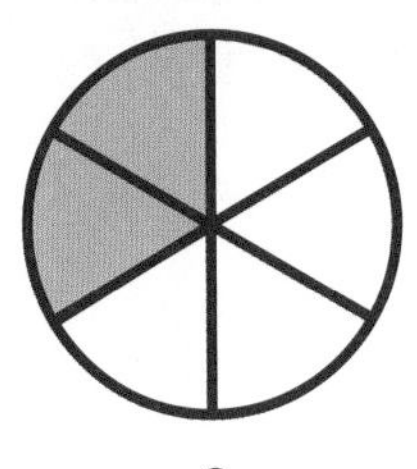
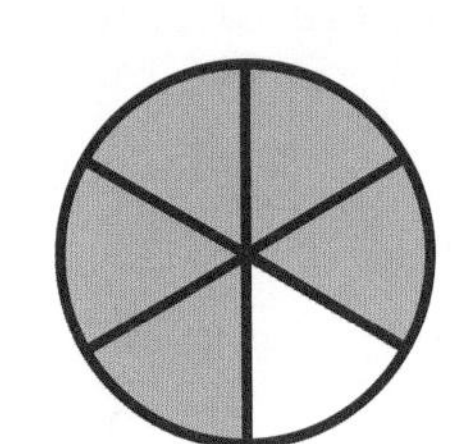
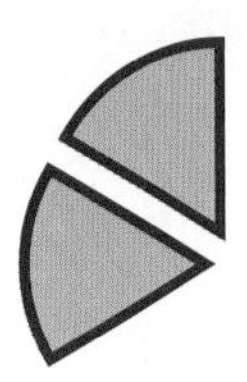

$\frac{2}{6} + \frac{5}{6} = \frac{7}{6}$

ADD the fractions and WRITE the sum.

1.

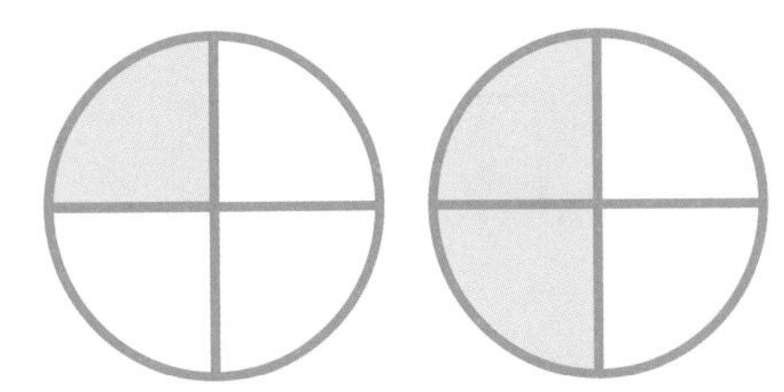

$\frac{1}{4} + \frac{2}{4} = \_\_$

2.

$\frac{5}{9} + \frac{2}{9} = \_\_$

3.

$\frac{5}{8} + \frac{5}{8} = \_\_$

4.

$\frac{1}{7} + \frac{6}{7} = \_\_$

5.

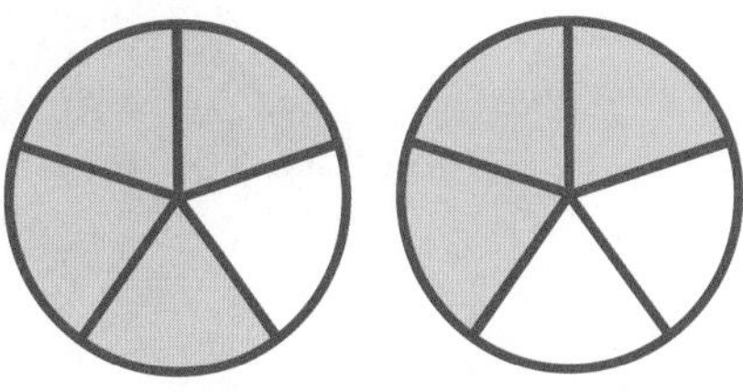

$\frac{4}{5} + \frac{3}{5} = \_\_$

6.

$\frac{3}{6} + \frac{2}{6} = \_\_$

More than One?

ADD the fractions. CIRCLE any sum that is greater than one.

HINT: A fraction is greater than one if the numerator is larger than the denominator.

1. $\frac{2}{6} + \frac{3}{6} = \frac{5}{6}$

2. $\frac{1}{3} + \frac{4}{3} = $ ___

3. $\frac{3}{10} + \frac{5}{10} = $ ___

4. $\frac{6}{9} + \frac{4}{9} = $ ___

5. $\frac{2}{7} + \frac{2}{7} = $ ___

6. $\frac{3}{5} + \frac{4}{5} = $ ___

7. $\frac{2}{4} + \frac{1}{4} = $ ___

8. $\frac{1}{2} + \frac{3}{2} = $ ___

9. $\frac{7}{12} + \frac{9}{12} = $ ___

10. $\frac{4}{6} + \frac{1}{6} = $ ___

11. $\frac{8}{11} + \frac{5}{11} = $ ___

12. $\frac{3}{8} + \frac{5}{8} = $ ___

Fraction Bars

When fractions have the same denominator, subtract them by subtracting the numerators only. The denominator stays the same.

Example:

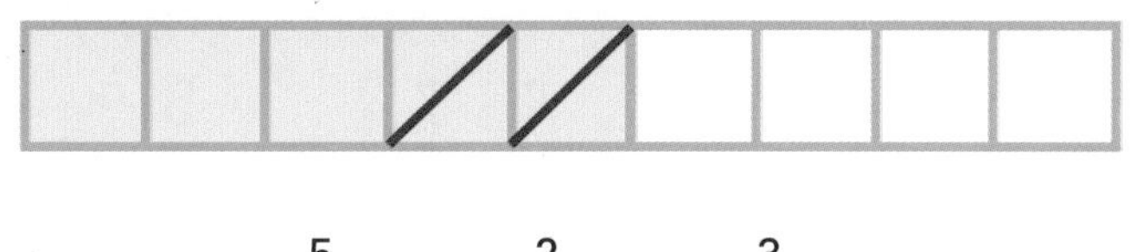

$\frac{5}{9} - \frac{2}{9} = \frac{3}{9}$

SUBTRACT the fractions and WRITE the difference.

HINT: Cross out the number of boxes of the second fraction to help you subtract.

1.

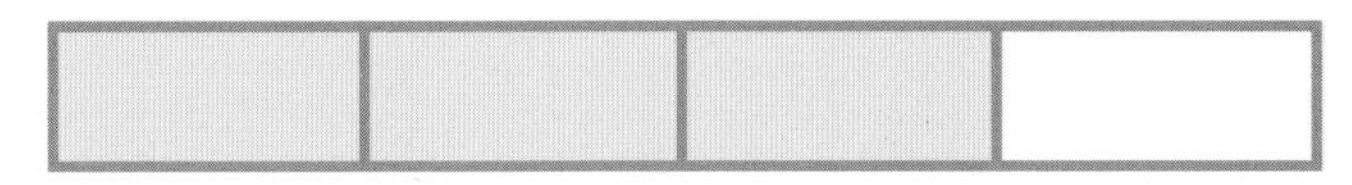

$\frac{3}{4} - \frac{1}{4} = \_\_\_$

2.

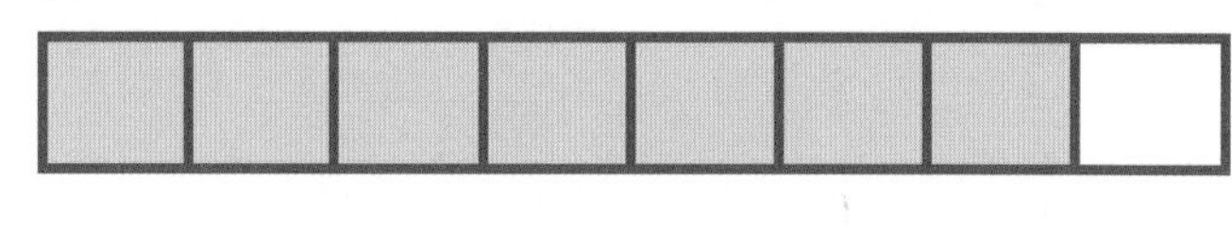

$\frac{7}{8} - \frac{2}{8} = \_\_\_$

3.

$\frac{6}{6} - \frac{5}{6} = \_\_\_$

4.

$\frac{4}{5} - \frac{1}{5} = \_\_\_$

5.

$\frac{10}{12} - \frac{4}{12} = \_\_\_$

6.

$\frac{6}{7} - \frac{3}{7} = \_\_\_$

Fraction Subtraction

WRITE each difference.

1. $\frac{4}{6} - \frac{3}{6} = \_\_\_$

2. $\frac{7}{8} - \frac{5}{8} = \_\_\_$

3. $\frac{2}{5} - \frac{1}{5} = \_\_\_$

4. $\frac{9}{10} - \frac{6}{10} = \_\_\_$

5. $\frac{5}{12} - \frac{2}{12} = \_\_\_$

6. $\frac{5}{7} - \frac{3}{7} = \_\_\_$

7. $\frac{8}{9} - \frac{4}{9} = \_\_\_$

8. $\frac{6}{4} - \frac{4}{4} = \_\_\_$

9. $\frac{8}{8} - \frac{2}{8} = \_\_\_$

10. $\frac{8}{5} - \frac{4}{5} = \_\_\_$

11. $\frac{5}{10} - \frac{1}{10} = \_\_\_$

12. $\frac{9}{6} - \frac{3}{6} = \_\_\_$

Tiny Tenths

This picture has $\frac{4}{10}$ shaded. In decimal form, this is written as 0.4.

ones	tenths
0 .	4

$\frac{4}{10}$ 0.4

WRITE the fraction and decimal for each picture.

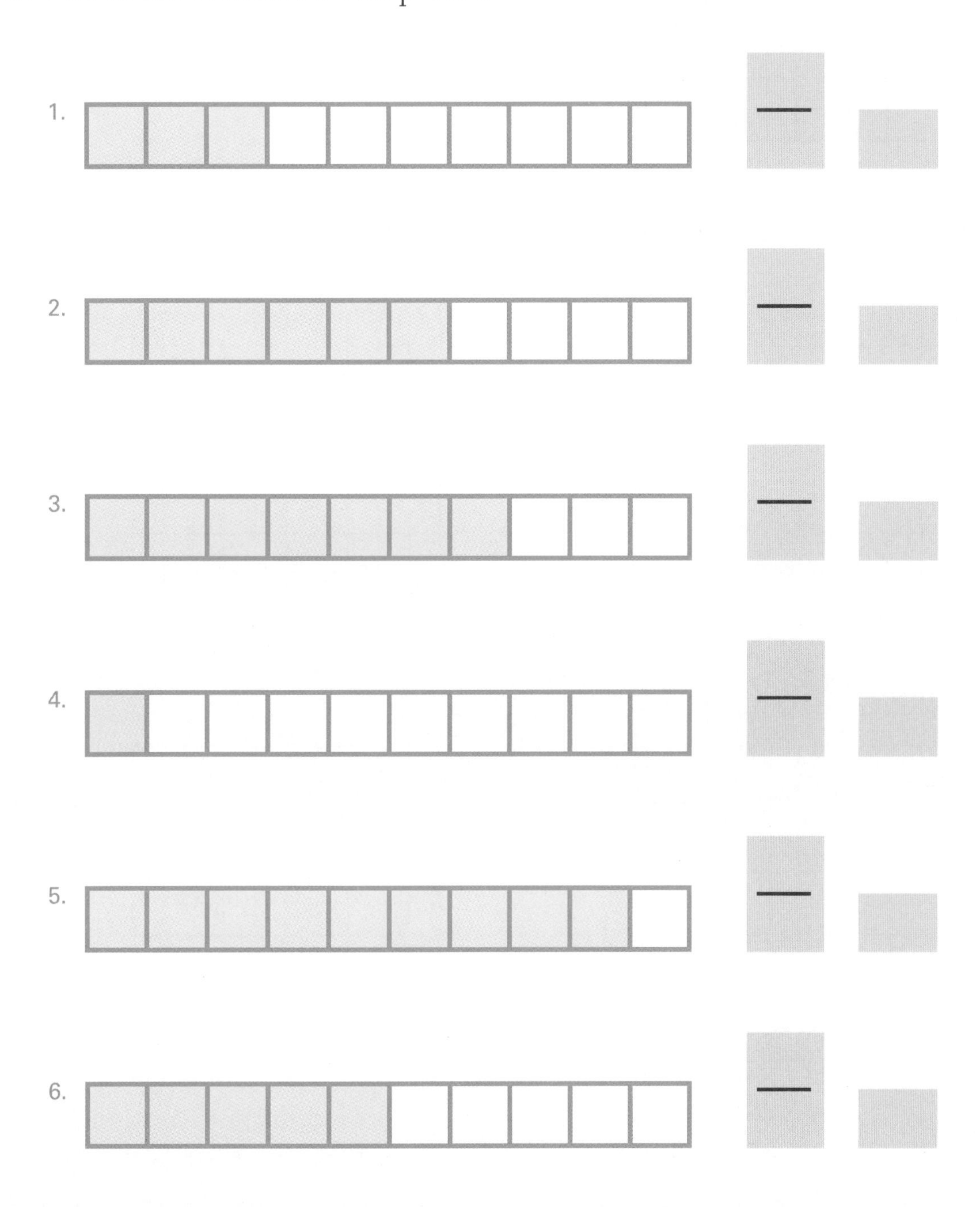

Handy Hundredths

This picture has $\frac{63}{100}$ shaded. In decimal form this is written as 0.63.

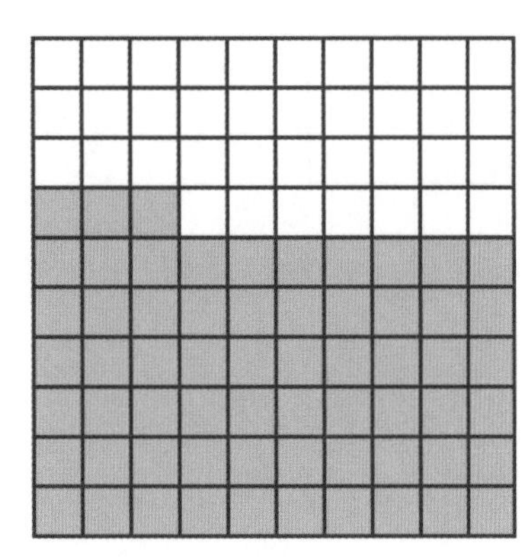

ones	tenths	hundredths
0	. 6	3

$\frac{63}{100}$ 0.63

WRITE the fraction and decimal for each picture.

1. 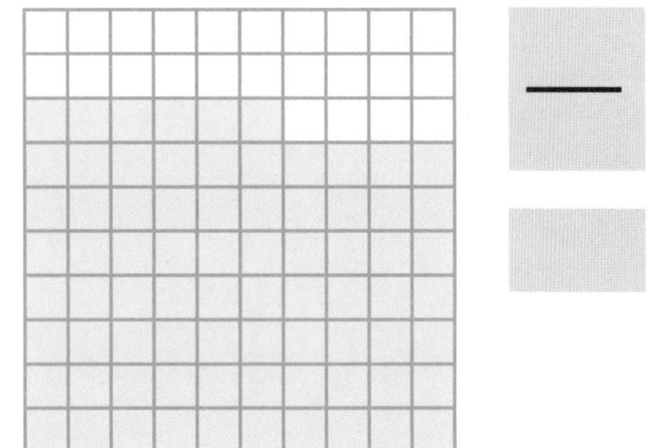

2. 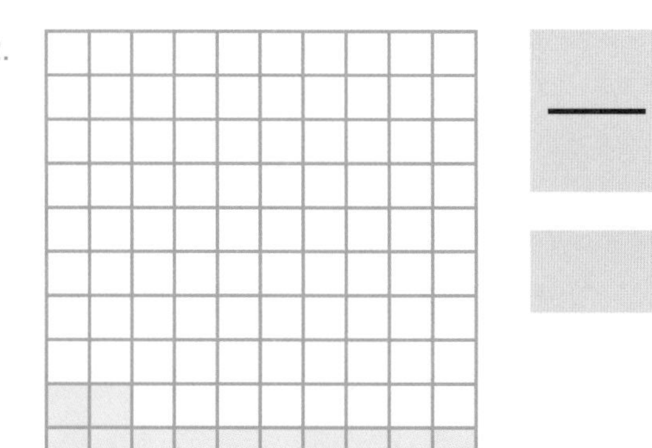

3. 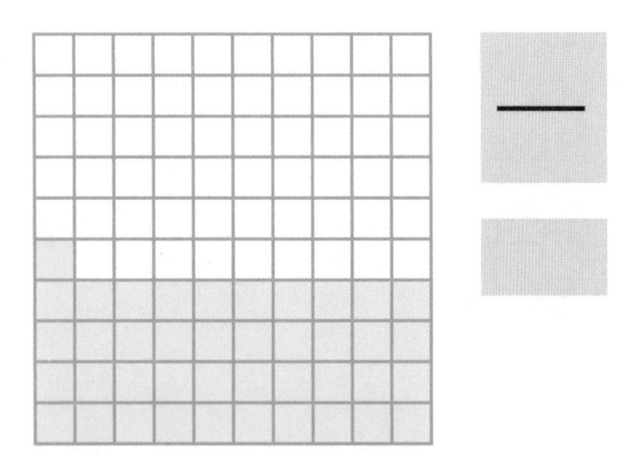

4. 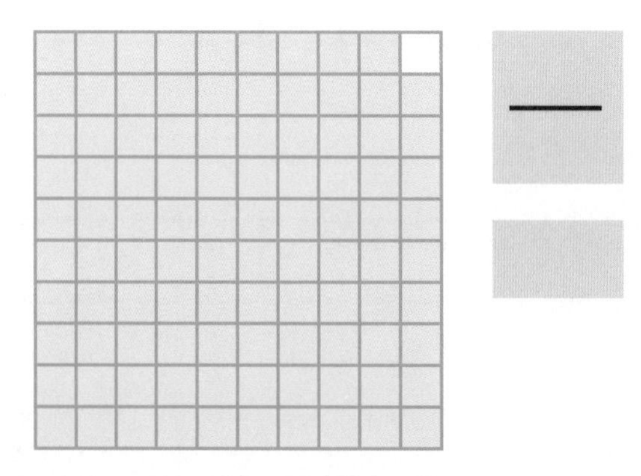

Cash Crunch

Decimals are used to represent dollars and cents. WRITE the value of the money in each row.

Example:   

$6.38

---

1.  

$ ________

---

2.    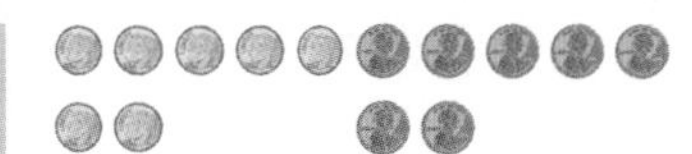

$ ________

---

3.  

$ ________

---

4. 

$ ________

---

5.    

$ ________

Get in Line

WRITE the missing numbers in each number line.

1.

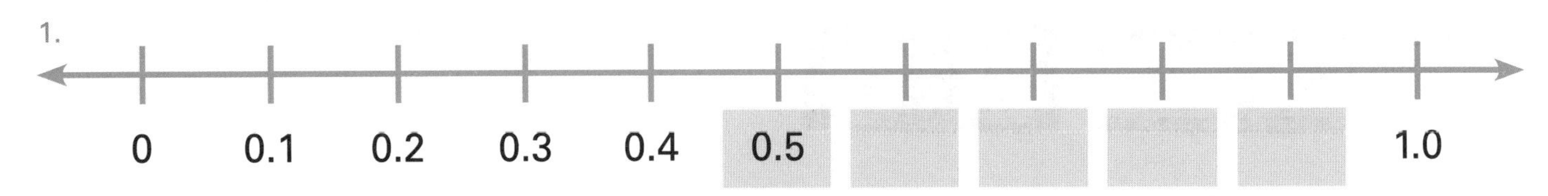

2.

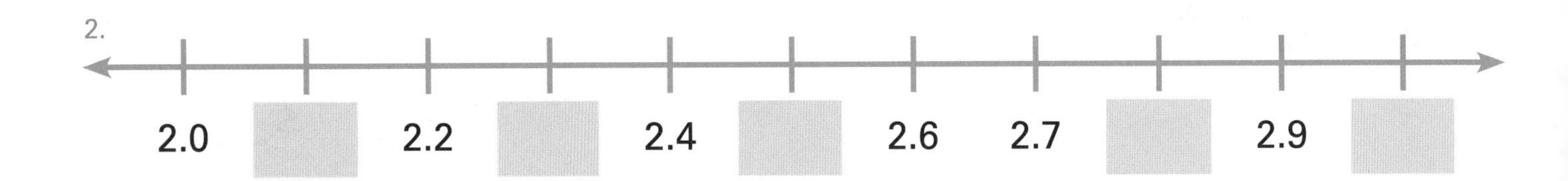

3.

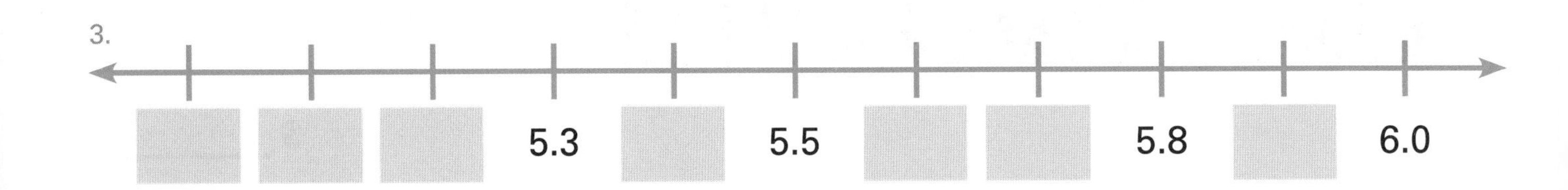

4.

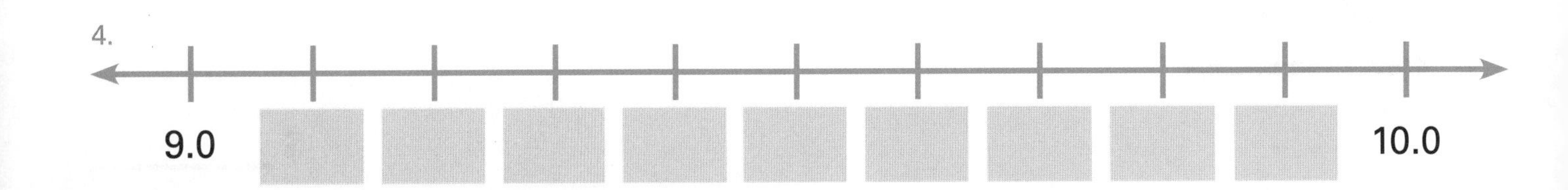

5.

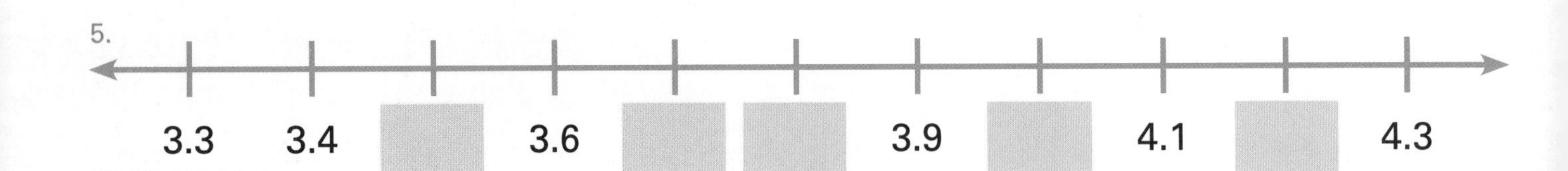

6.

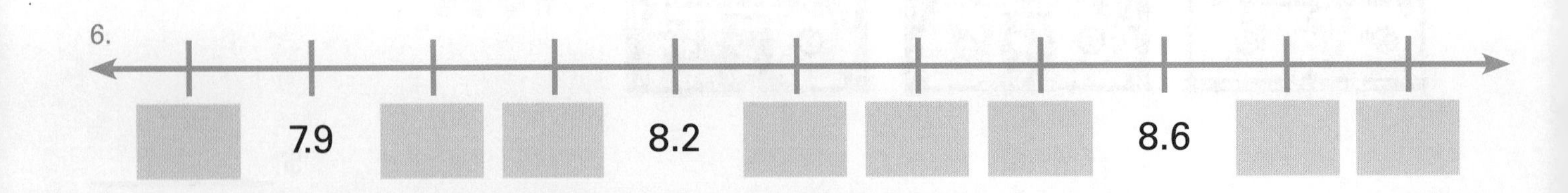

Color and Compare

COLOR the picture to match each decimal. Then CIRCLE the smaller decimal.

0.5

0.3

0.2

0.8

0.9

0.7

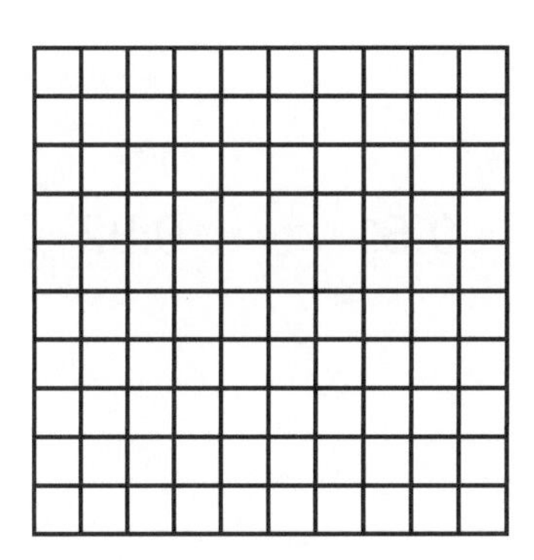

0.68

0.93

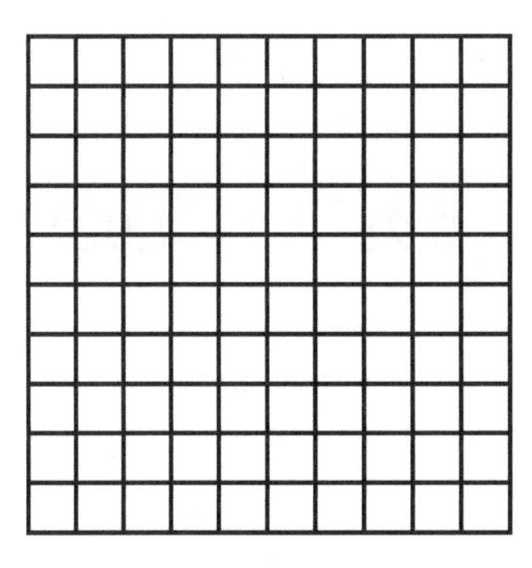

0.46

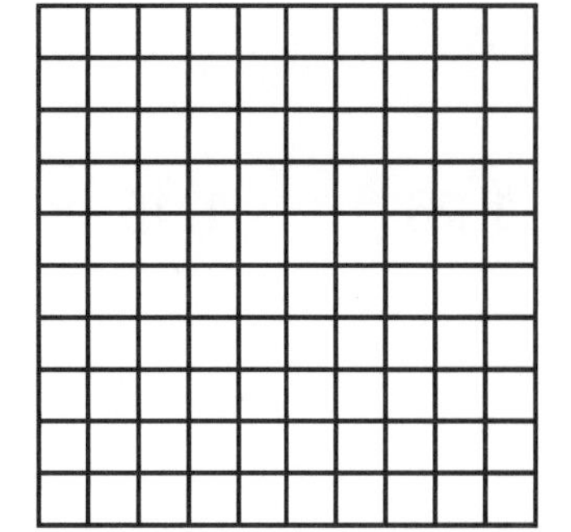

0.42

Matched or Mismatched?

COMPARE each pair of decimals, and WRITE >, <, or = in the box.

Example: 0.4 < 0.6

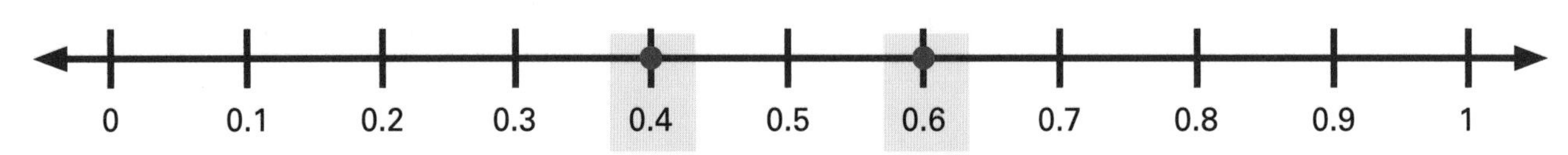

0.2 ☐ 0.8 (1)	0.6 ☐ 0.5 (2)	0.1 ☐ 0.2 (3)	0.4 ☐ 0.7 (4)
1.4 ☐ 1.2 (5)	1.3 ☐ 1.7 (6)	1.8 ☐ 1.8 (7)	1.0 ☐ 0.9 (8)
0.34 ☐ 0.27 (9)	0.42 ☐ 0.42 (10)	0.56 ☐ 0.61 (11)	0.92 ☐ 0.90 (12)
1.55 ☐ 1.59 (13)	0.98 ☐ 1.89 (14)	0.76 ☐ 0.96 (15)	1.21 ☐ 1.21 (16)
0.96 ☐ 1.26 (17)	1.45 ☐ 1.31 (18)	0.26 ☐ 0.25 (19)	1.02 ☐ 1.01 (20)

Cash Crunch

ADD the dollar amounts.

Example:

```
  $10.54
+  6.12
  $16.66
```

1.
```
  $14.63
+   3.20
  $
```

2.
```
  $22.01
+   5.78
  $
```

3.
```
  $44.82
+   2.11
  $
```

4.
```
  $28.31
+ 11.42
  $
```

5.
```
  $10.93
+ 42.04
  $
```

6.
```
  $52.08
+ 16.30
  $
```

7.
```
  $852.61
+   13.14
  $
```

8.
```
  $162.20
+   25.74
  $
```

9.
```
  $734.12
+   51.40
  $
```

10.
```
  $418.16
+ 150.03
  $
```

11.
```
  $331.04
+ 311.24
  $
```

12.
```
  $243.24
+ 753.21
  $
```

Cash Crunch

SUBTRACT the dollar amounts.

Example:

$21.57
−11.36
$10.21

1. $17.82
− 2.51
$

2. $64.32
− 4.12
$

3. $79.57
− 8.21
$

4. $31.99
−20.96
$

5. $13.84
−10.72
$

6. $81.76
−41.06
$

7. $368.62
− 37.02
$

8. $592.63
− 71.42
$

9. $454.66
− 20.53
$

10. $266.74
−103.52
$

11. $917.88
−312.21
$

12. $186.73
−135.43
$

It All Adds Up

When adding decimals, add and regroup as you normally would, keeping the decimal between the ones place and the tenths place.

Step 1	Step 2	Step 3	Step 4
1 53.85 + 67.56 1	1 1 53.85 + 67.56 .41	11 1 53.85 + 67.56 1.41	11 1 53.85 + 67.56 121.41
Add the hundredths. 5 + 6 = 11	Add the tenths. 1 + 8 + 5 = 14	Add the ones. 1 + 3 + 7 = 11	Add the tens. 1 + 5 + 6 = 12

ADD each sum.

1. 7.5 + 0.9

2. 3.21 + 9.29

3. 81.94 + 8.83

4. 28.53 + 99.58

5. 11.76 + 59.86

6. 27.36 + 88.25

7. 575.07 + 71.86

8. 448.86 + 58.58

9. 199.69 + 90.70

10. 197.45 + 424.91

11. 514.37 + 382.84

12. 347.79 + 132.46

What's the Difference?

When subtracting decimals, subtract and regroup as you normally would, keeping the decimal between the ones place and the tenths place.

0 16 83.16 − 16.37 9	2 10 16 83.16 − 16.37 .79	7 12 10 16 83.16 − 16.37 6.79	7 12 10 16 83.16 − 16.37 66.79
Subtract the hundredths. 16 − 7 = 9	Subtract the tenths. 10 − 3 = 7	Subtract the ones. 12 − 6 = 6	Subtract the tens. 7 − 1 = 6

WRITE each difference.

1. 6.4 − 3.5

2. 4.72 − 1.16

3. 33.56 − 4.28

4. 52.1 − 11.4

5. 63.18 − 44.26

6. 32.37 − 16.49

7. 848.08 − 77.41

8. 103.98 − 64.72

9. 282.45 − 53.94

10. 690.90 − 131.45

11. 353.42 − 262.24

12. 936.65 − 573.79

Unit Rewind

WRITE the fraction.

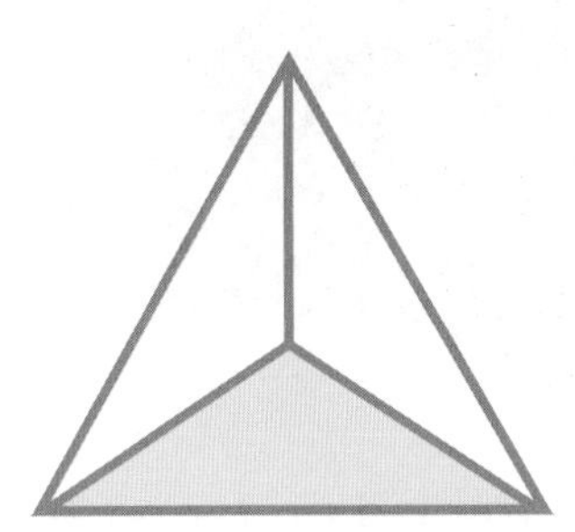

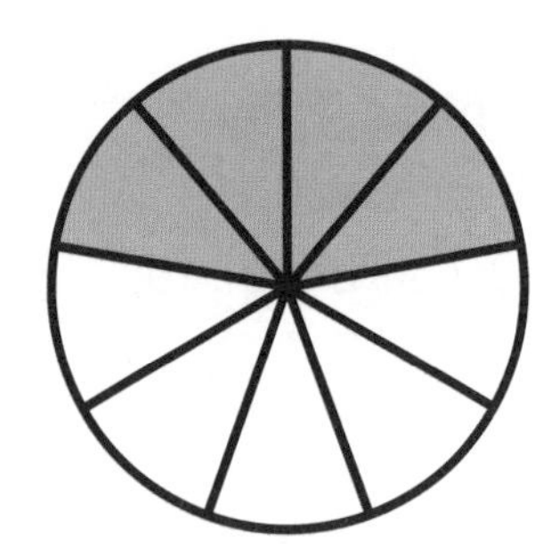

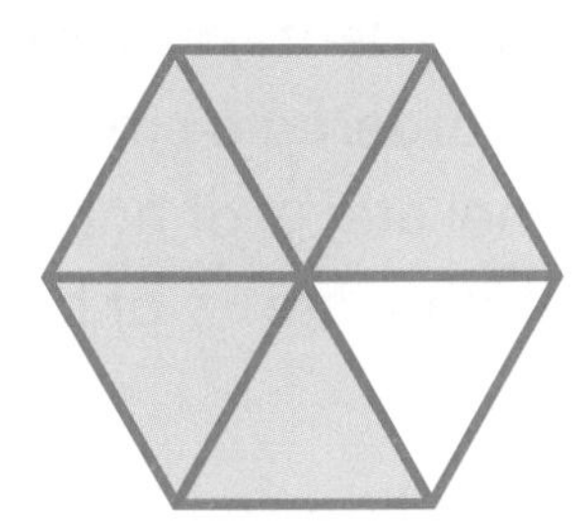

1

2

3

WRITE each decimal.

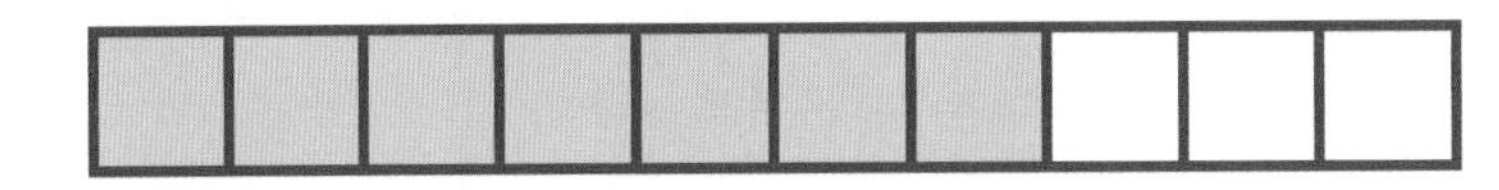

4

5

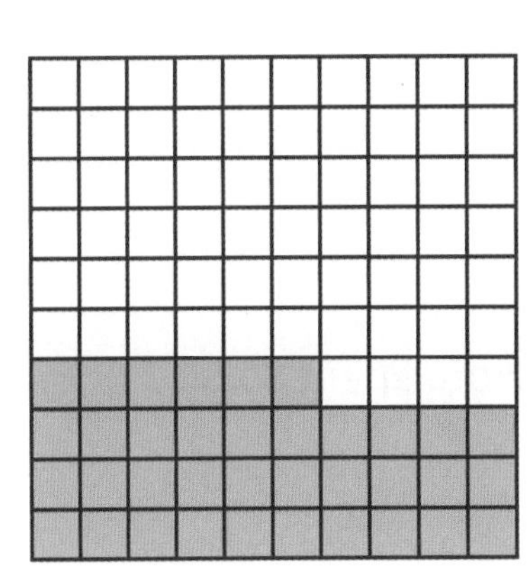

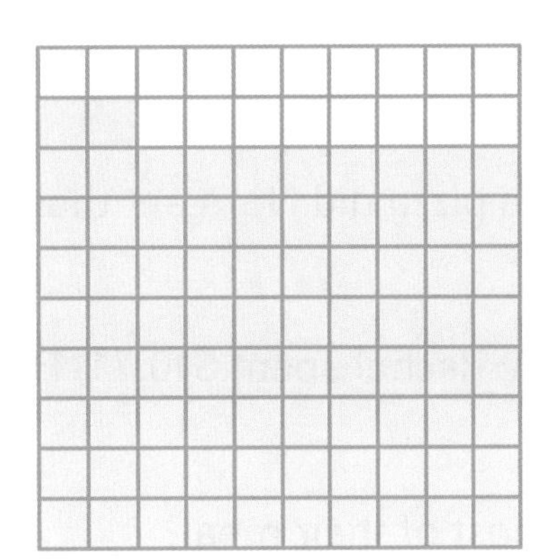

6

7

Work It Out

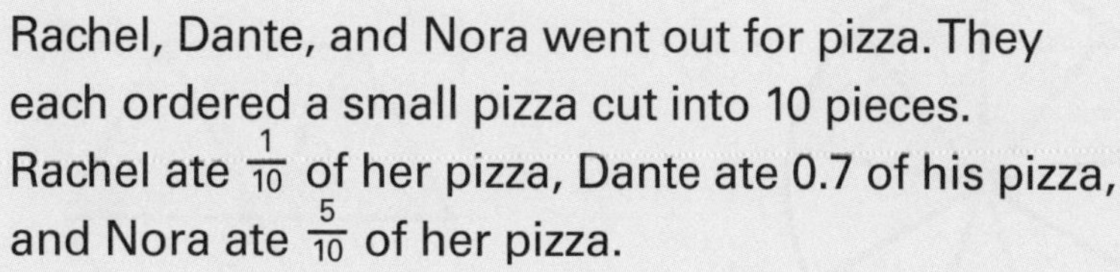

Rachel, Dante, and Nora went out for pizza. They each ordered a small pizza cut into 10 pieces. Rachel ate $\frac{1}{10}$ of her pizza, Dante ate 0.7 of his pizza, and Nora ate $\frac{5}{10}$ of her pizza.

1. Each of these pizzas belongs to one of the kids. WRITE the name of the kid under each pizza.

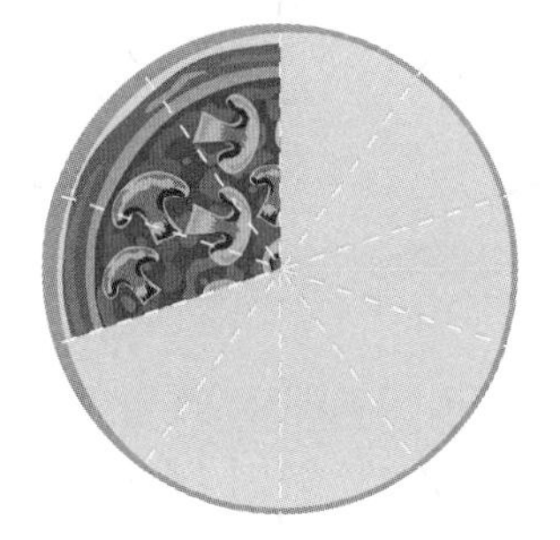

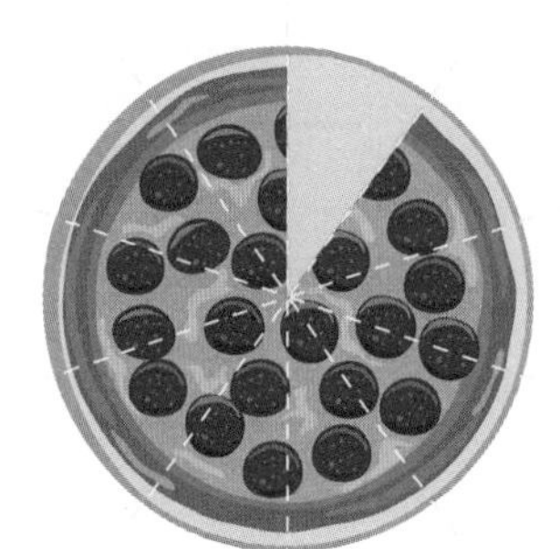

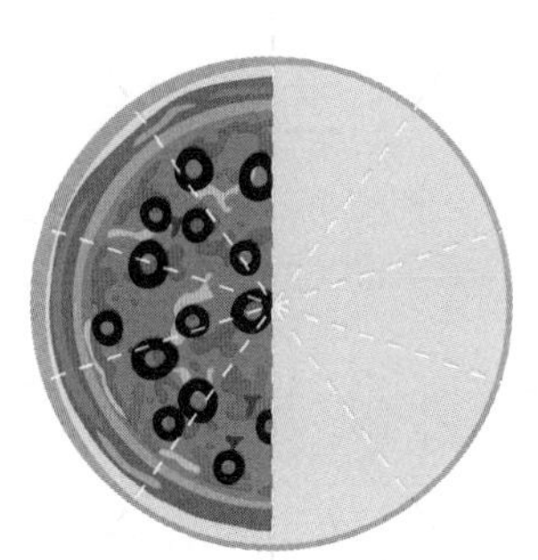

______________ ______________ ______________

2. If Dante and Nora's leftovers were combined, what fraction of a pizza would there be? __________

3. How much more of a pizza did Nora eat than Rachel? __________

With drinks and dessert, Rachel spent $10.71, Dante spent $11.23, and Nora spent $9.88.

4. What was the total cost of their meal? __________

Unit Rewind

WRITE >, <, or = in each box.

1. $\frac{5}{5}$ ☐ $\frac{2}{2}$

2. $\frac{1}{7}$ ☐ $\frac{1}{12}$

3. $\frac{2}{3}$ ☐ $\frac{6}{3}$

4. $\frac{3}{8}$ ☐ $\frac{2}{9}$

5. $\frac{4}{7}$ ☐ $\frac{5}{7}$

6. $\frac{3}{6}$ ☐ $\frac{4}{8}$

7. $\frac{3}{5}$ ☐ $\frac{5}{12}$

8. $\frac{2}{6}$ ☐ $\frac{6}{2}$

WRITE each sum.

9. $\frac{1}{6} + \frac{4}{6} = \_\_\_$

10. $\frac{3}{7} + \frac{1}{7} = \_\_\_$

11. $\frac{3}{5} + \frac{3}{5} = \_\_\_$

12. $\frac{1}{4} + \frac{1}{4} = \_\_\_$

13. $\frac{8}{10} + \frac{3}{10} = \_\_\_$

14. $\frac{2}{3} + \frac{1}{3} = \_\_\_$

WRITE each difference.

15. $\frac{7}{9} - \frac{3}{9} = \_\_\_$

16. $\frac{3}{5} - \frac{1}{5} = \_\_\_$

17. $\frac{5}{8} - \frac{2}{8} = \_\_\_$

18. $\frac{10}{10} - \frac{5}{10} = \_\_\_$

19. $\frac{6}{7} - \frac{2}{7} = \_\_\_$

20. $\frac{9}{12} - \frac{8}{12} = \_\_\_$

Unit Rewind

WRITE >, <, or = in each box.

0.2 ☐ 0.7 (1)	1.2 ☐ 1.2 (2)	0.8 ☐ 0.6 (3)	12.2 ☐ 11.9 (4)
1.52 ☐ 1.16 (5)	3.85 ☐ 4.02 (6)	6.55 ☐ 6.55 (7)	4.89 ☐ 4.9 (8)

WRITE each sum.

9. 1.2 + 0.6 = ______
10. 3.1 + 1.5 = ______
11. 5.22 + 2.11 = ______

12. 28.25 + 48.66 = ______
13. 159.99 + 26.13 = ______
14. 392.59 + 271.93 = ______

WRITE each difference.

15. 1.9 − 0.4 = ______
16. 6.4 − 1.1 = ______
17. 7.96 − 4.25 = ______

18. 50.97 − 22.92 = ______
19. 482.35 − 55.64 = ______
20. 627.53 − 334.53 = ______

Measure Up

MEASURE the length of each object in centimeters (cm).

1 centimeter is made up of 10 millimeters (mm).

Example:

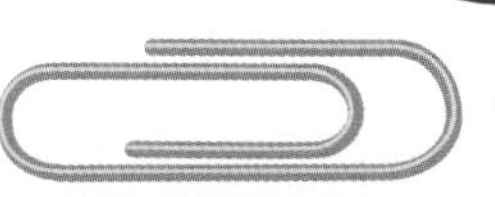

WRITE each answer as a decimal.

1. ______ cm

2. ______ cm

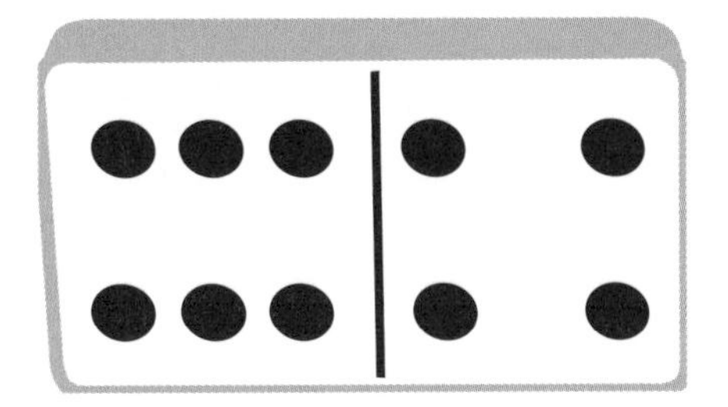

3. ______ cm

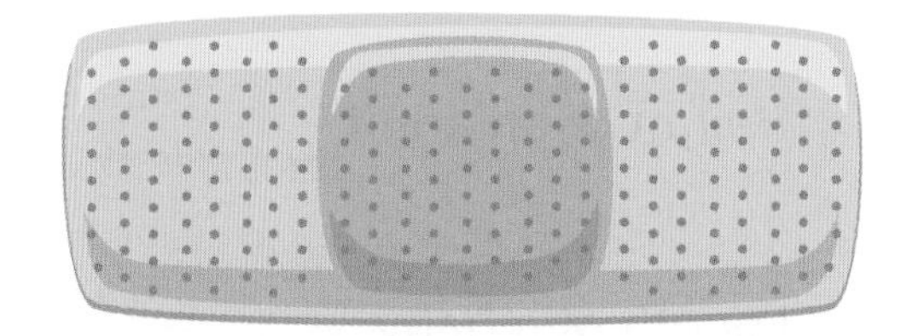

4. ______ cm

5. ______ cm

Preferred Measure

Which unit of measure would you use to measure the length of each object? WRITE *mm*, *cm*, *m*, or *km*.

1 centimeter (cm) = 10 millimeters (mm)

1 mm 1 cm

NOTE: These lines show how these units compare to each other. They are not actual size.

1 meter (m) = 100 centimeters

1 cm 1 m

1 kilometer (km) = 1,000 meters

1 m 1 km

1. Distance from Chicago to Toronto ______
2. Height of an adult ______
3. Length of a baby ______
4. Size of an ant ______
5. Distance of a 30-second run ______
6. Distance of a 30-minute run ______
7. Height of a basketball hoop ______
8. Size of a pencil ______

Measuring Mash-up

WRITE the equivalent measurement.

1 centimeter (cm) = 10 millimeters (mm)

1 meter (m) = 100 centimeters

1 kilometer (km) = 1,000 meters

Examples:

5 km = 5,000 m	1 kilometer = 1,000 meters	5 × 1,000 = 5,000
300 cm = 3 m	100 centimeters = 1 meter	300 ÷ 100 = 3

1. 6 m = _______ cm
2. 12 cm = _______ mm
3. 10 km = _______ m
4. 30 mm = _______ cm
5. 2,500 cm = _______ m
6. 25 cm = _______ mm
7. 6,000 m = _______ km
8. 46 m = _______ cm
9. 90 mm = _______ cm
10. 50 cm = _______ m
11. 8 mm = _______ cm
12. $\frac{1}{2}$ km = _______ m

What's Longest?

CIRCLE the longest measurement in each row.

1 centimeter (cm) = 10 millimeters (mm)

1 meter (m) = 100 centimeters

1 kilometer (km) = 1,000 meters

1.	1 m	1 cm	1 km	1 mm
2.	14 mm	2 m	7 cm	5 cm
3.	1 m	200 cm	250 mm	96 cm
4.	40 m	4,000 mm	400 cm	4 mm
5.	2 km	2,500 cm	25 mm	2,500 m
6.	400 cm	5 m	6,000 mm	3 m

Measure Up

MEASURE the length of each object in inches (in.). WRITE each answer as a fraction.

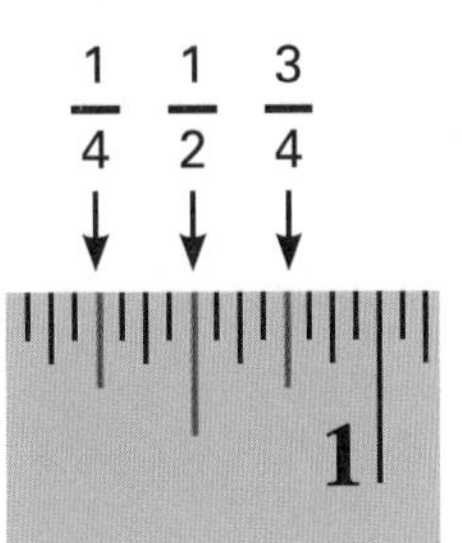

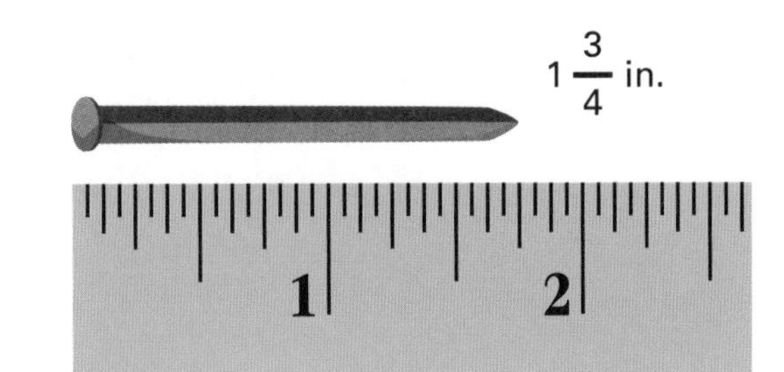

1. ______ in.

2. ______ in.

3. ______ in.

4. ______ in.

5. ______ in.

Preferred Measure

Which unit of measure would you use to measure the length of each object? WRITE *in.*, *ft*, *yd*, or *mi*.

1 foot (ft) = 12 inches

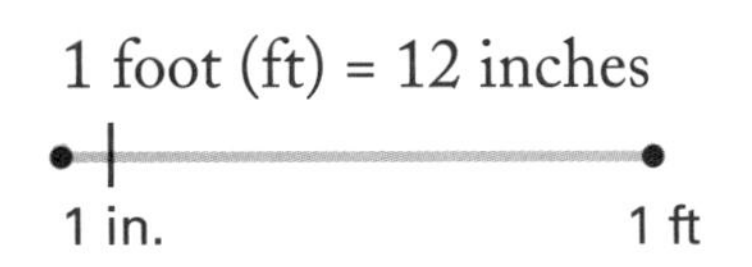

NOTE: These lines show how these units compare to each other. They are not actual size.

1 yard (yd) = 3 feet

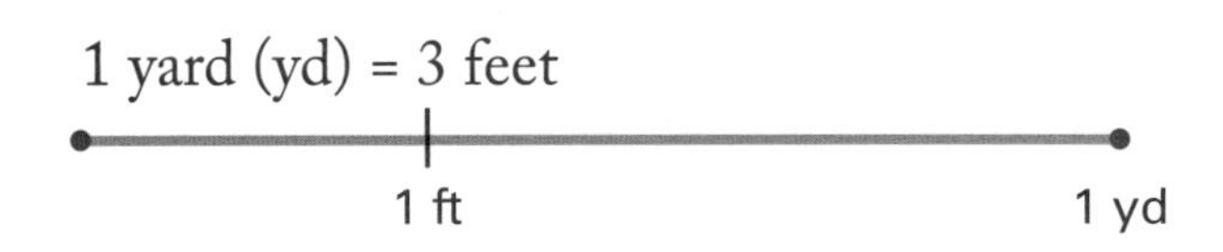

1 mile (mi) = 1,760 yards or 5,280 feet

1 yd 1 mi

1. Height of a coffee mug _______
2. Length of a football field _______
3. Height of a room _______
4. Distance from New York to Los Angeles _______
5. Length of a caterpillar _______
6. Distance across a small lake _______
7. Distance across the Pacific Ocean _______
8. Depth of a swimming pool _______

Measuring Mash-up

WRITE the equivalent measurement.

1 foot (ft) = 12 inches

1 yard (yd) = 3 feet

1 mile (mi) = 1,760 yards or 5,280 feet

Examples:

15 yd = 45 ft	1 yard = 3 feet	$15 \times 3 = 45$
24 in. = 2 ft	12 inches = 1 foot	$24 \div 12 = 2$

1. 2 ft = ______ in.
2. 36 in. = ______ ft
3. 1 yd = ______ in.
4. 3 mi = ______ yd
5. 24 yd = ______ ft
6. 3,520 yd = ______ mi
7. 52 ft = ______ in.
8. 2 mi = ______ ft
9. 336 in. = ______ ft
10. 72 in. = ______ yd
11. 6 in. = ______ ft
12. 1 ft = ______ yd

What's the Shortest?

CIRCLE the shortest measurement in each row.

1 foot (ft) = 12 inches

1 yard (yd) = 3 feet

1 mile (mi) = 1,760 yards or 5,280 feet

1.	1 mi	1 in.	1 yd	1 ft
2.	4 yd	5 mi	2 ft	26 in.
3.	40 in.	3 yd	2 mi	16 ft
4.	2,000 yd	1 mi	6,200 ft	1,729 yd
5.	180 in.	16 ft	6 yd	21 ft
6.	41 yd	6 mi	1, 445 in.	120 ft

Squared Away

Perimeter is the distance around a two-dimensional shape. **Area** is the size of the surface of a shape, and it is measured in square units.

To measure the **perimeter**, count the number of units on the outside of the rectangle.

To measure the **area**, count the number of square units.

The perimeter of this rectangle is 10 units.

The area of this rectangle is 6 square units.

1 square unit

WRITE the perimeter and area of each shape.

1.

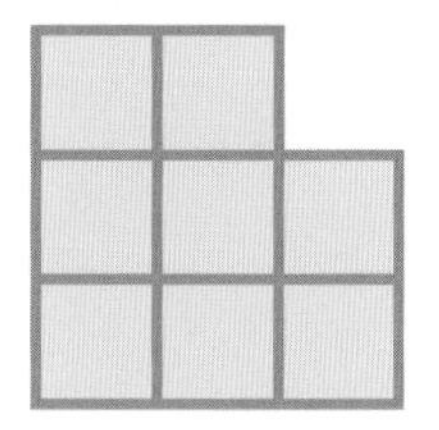

Perimeter: ________ units

Area: ________ square units

2.

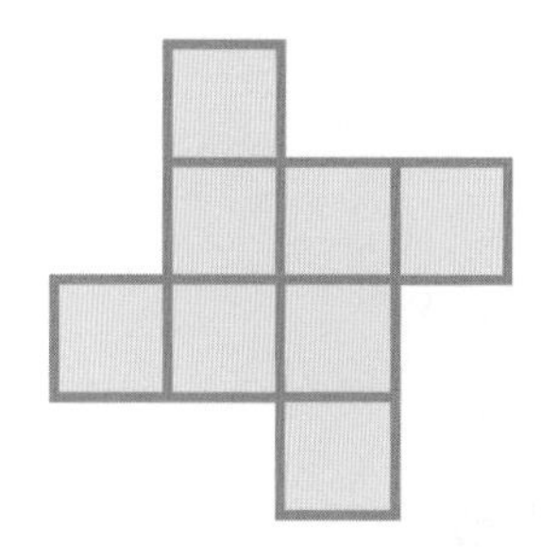

Perimeter: ________ units

Area: ________ square units

3.

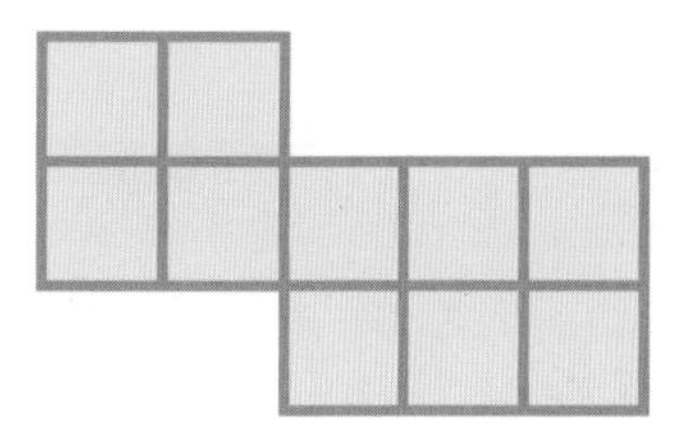

Perimeter: ________ units

Area: ________ square units

4.

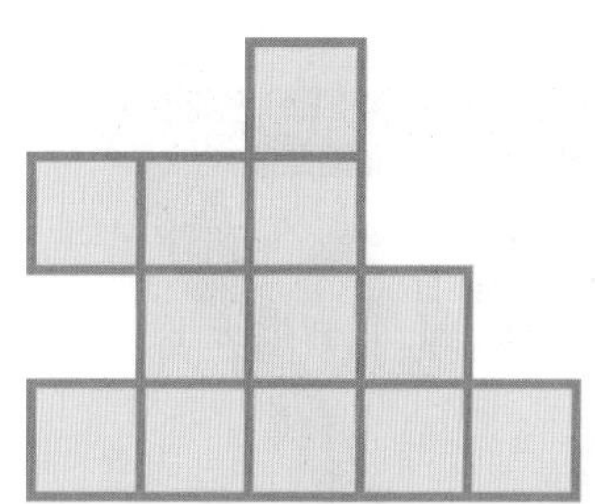

Perimeter: ________ units

Area: ________ square units

Around We Go

Find the perimeter by adding the length of every side.

30 in.

24 in.

$24 + 30 + 24 + 30 = 108$ in.

WRITE the perimeter of each shape.

10 in.

5 in.

24 in.

1. ______ in.

2. ______ in.

36 in.

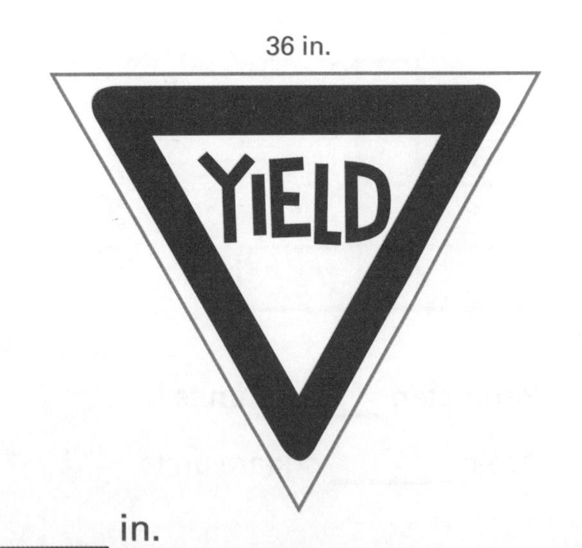

12 in.

36 in.

3. ______ in.

4. ______ in.

Frame Up

Find the area of a rectangle by multiplying the length by the width. WRITE the area of each shape.

Example: 18 cm × 23 cm = 414 square centimeters (sq cm)

15 cm

10 cm

1. ______ sq cm

19 cm

24 cm

2. ______ sq cm

46 cm

36 cm

3. ______ sq cm

16 cm

16 cm

4. ______ sq cm

Rulers Rule

MEASURE each rectangle in centimeters. WRITE the perimeter and area of each shape.

1.

Perimeter: ______ cm

Area: ______ sq cm

2.

Perimeter: ______ cm

Area: ______ sq cm

3.

Perimeter: ______ cm

Area: ______ sq cm

Preferred Measure

Which unit of measure would you use to measure the weight of each object? WRITE *oz*, *lb*, or *T*.

Examples:

1 ounce (oz)

1 pound (lb)
1 pound = 16 ounces

1 ton (T)
1 ton = 2,000 pounds

1. Weight of a hippopotamus _______

2. Weight of a person _______

3. Weight of a box of macaroni and cheese _______

4. Weight of a dump truck _______

5. Weight of a lemon _______

6. Weight of a bag of groceries _______

7. Weight of a sailboat _______

8. Weight of a plate _______

Weigh In

Each weight is shown in pounds. WRITE each weight in ounces.

HINT: One pound equals 16 ounces, so multiply each weight by 16.

1. ________ oz

2. ________ oz

3. ________ oz

4. ________ oz

Measuring Mash-up

WRITE the equivalent measurement.

1 pound (lb) = 16 ounces (oz)

1 ton (T) = 2,000 pounds

Examples:

3T = 6,000 lb	1 ton = 2,000 pounds	3 × 2,000 = 6,000
48 oz = 3 lb	16 ounces = 1 pound	48 ÷ 16 = 3

1. 32 oz = ______ lb
2. 4,000 lb = ______ T
3. 14 lb = ______ oz
4. 4 T = ______ lb
5. 50 lb = ______ oz
6. 192 oz = ______ lb
7. 20,000 lb = ______ T
8. 6 T = ______ lb
9. 100 lb = ______ oz
10. $\frac{1}{2}$ T = ______ lb
11. $\frac{1}{4}$ lb = ______ oz
12. $\frac{1}{2}$ lb = ______ oz

The Mighty Marlock

The Mighty Marlock will guess any weight, but he sometimes guesses incorrectly. CROSS OUT any picture where his guess is likely wrong.

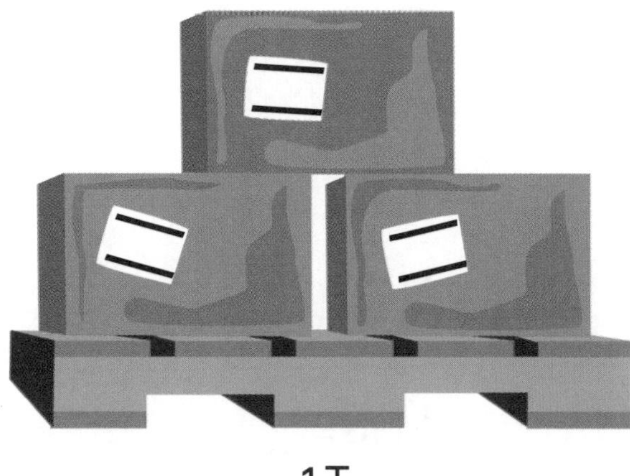

1 T

12 oz

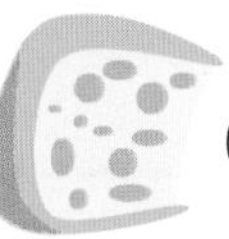

6 oz

4 T

300 lb

8 lb

Preferred Measure

Which unit of measure would you use to measure the weight of each object? WRITE *mg*, *g*, or *kg*.

1 gram = 1,000 milligrams

1 kilogram = 1,000 grams

Examples:

1 milligram (1 mg)

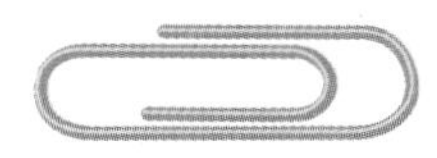
1 gram (1 g)

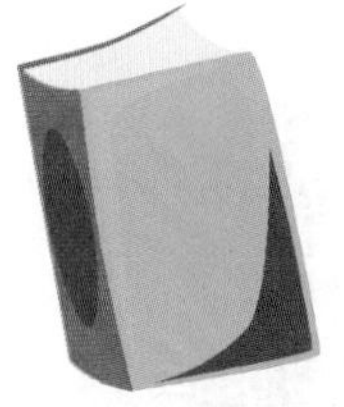
1 kilogram (1 kg)

1. Weight of a pen ______
2. Weight of a lion ______
3. Weight of some sugar crystals ______
4. Weight of a sugar cube ______
5. Weight of a baby ______
6. Weight of a small piece of yarn ______
7. Weight of a remote control ______
8. Weight of a toothbrush ______

Weigh In

Each weight is shown in kilograms. WRITE each weight in grams.

1 kilogram = 1,000 grams

0.5 kilograms = 500 grams

0.1 kilograms = 100 grams

_____ g
1

_____ g
2

_____ g
3

_____ g
4

Measuring Mash-up

WRITE the equivalent measurement.

1 gram (g) = 1,000 milligrams (mg)

1 kilogram (kg) = 1,000 grams

Examples:

4 kg = 4,000 g	1 kilogram = 1,000 grams	4 × 1,000 = 4,000
3,000 mg = 3 g	1,000 milligrams = 1 gram	3,000 ÷ 1,000 = 3

1. 2 kg = ______ g
2. 6,000 g = ______ kg
3. 2,000 mg = ______ g
4. 0.1 kg = ______ g
5. 12 g = ______ mg
6. 10,000 g = ______ kg
7. 5,000 mg = ______ g
8. 0.5 g = ______ mg
9. 600 g = ______ kg
10. 400 g = ______ kg
11. 100 mg = ______ g
12. 2.3 kg = ______ g

The Mighty Marlock

The Mighty Marlock will guess any weight, but he sometimes guesses incorrectly. CROSS OUT any picture where his guess is likely wrong.

3 g

800 mg

7 mg

5 kg

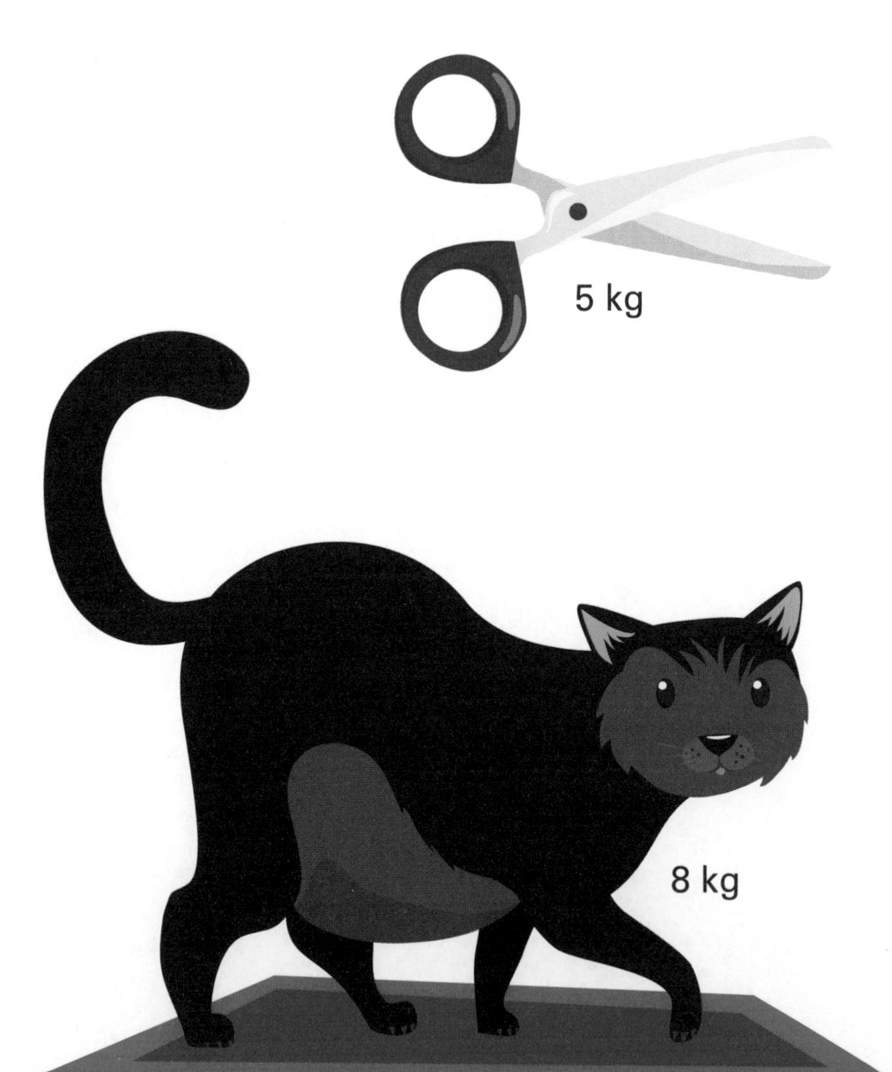

8 kg

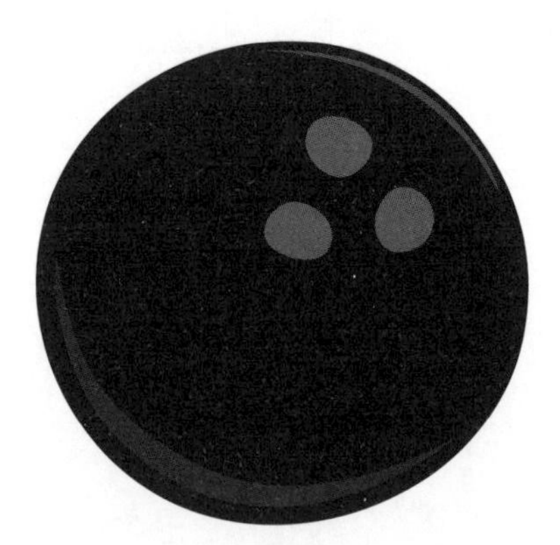

75 g

Measure Up

MEASURE the length of each piece of licorice in centimeters. WRITE each answer as a decimal.

1. ______ cm

2. ______ cm

3. ______ cm

MEASURE the length of each piece of ribbon in inches. WRITE each answer as a fraction.

4. ______ in.

5. ______ in.

6. ______ in.

Squared Away

WRITE the area and perimeter of each shape.

1. Perimeter: _______ units

Area: _______ square units

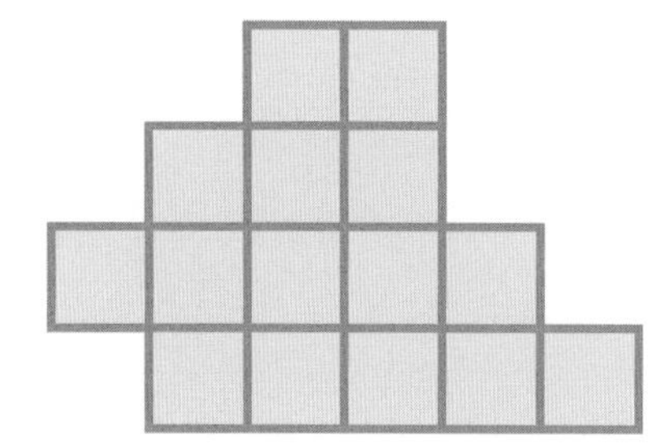

2. Perimeter: _______ ft

Area: _______ sq ft

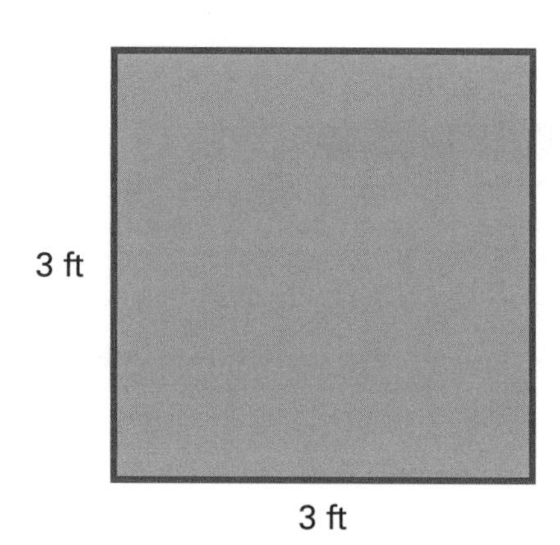

3. Perimeter: _______ cm

Area: _______ sq cm

7 cm

14 cm

4. Perimeter: _______ yd

Area: _______ sq yd

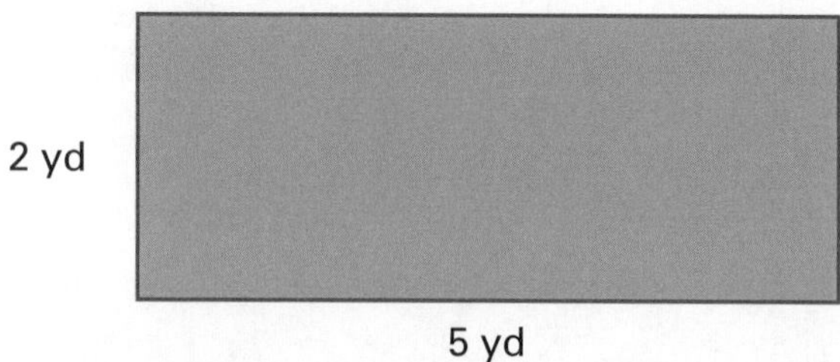

Preferred Measure

CIRCLE the unit of measure you would use for each object.

1.	Weight of a penny	gram	kilogram	milligram
2.	Height of a wall	inch	mile	foot
3.	Weight of a hippopotamus	ton	pound	ounce
4.	Length of a belt	yard	inch	mile
5.	Distance of a marathon	foot	inch	mile
6.	Weight of an eyelash	milligram	kilogram	gram
7.	Weight of a backpack	gram	milligram	kilogram
8.	Length of a worm	kilometer	centimeter	meter

Measuring Mash-up

WRITE the equivalent measurement.

1 centimeter (cm) = 10 millimeters (mm)

1 meter (m) = 100 centimeters

1 kilometer (km) = 1,000 meters

1 foot (ft) = 12 inches

1 yard (yd) = 3 feet

1 mile (mi) = 1,760 yards or 5,280 feet

1 gram (g) = 1,000 milligrams (mg)

1 kilogram (kg) = 1,000 grams

1 pound (lb) = 16 ounces (oz)

1 ton (T) = 2,000 pounds

1. 24 lb = ______ oz
2. 80 yd = ______ ft
3. 15 g = ______ mg
4. 900 cm = ______ m
5. 8,000 lb = ______ T
6. 144 in = ______ ft
7. 0.5 m = ______ cm
8. $\frac{1}{2}$ mi = ______ yd
9. 0.7 kg = ______ g
10. 80 oz = ______ lb
11. 6,000 mg = ______ g
12. 3,520 yd = ______ mi
13. 5 T = ______ lb
14. 4 oz = ______ lb
15. 150 cm = ______ m

Angle Untangle

An **angle** is formed when two lines meet, and it is measured in degrees using a protractor. There are three different types of angles: right, acute, and obtuse.

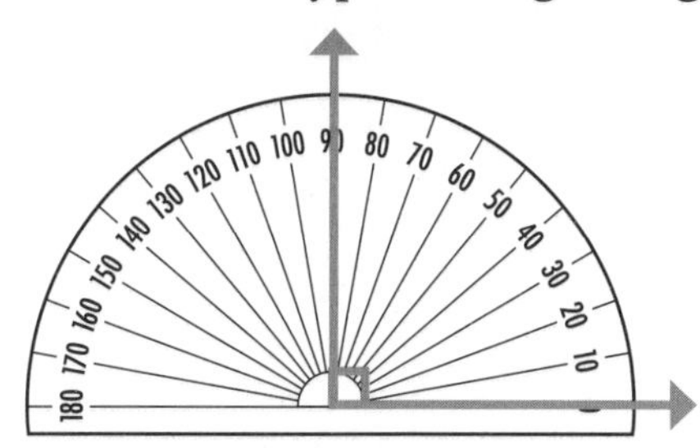

A **right** angle is an angle measuring exactly 90°, indicated by the ⌉ symbol in the corner.

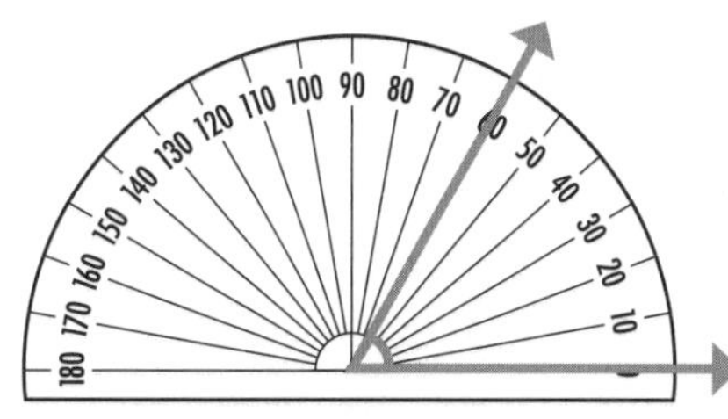

An **acute** angle is any angle measuring less than 90°.

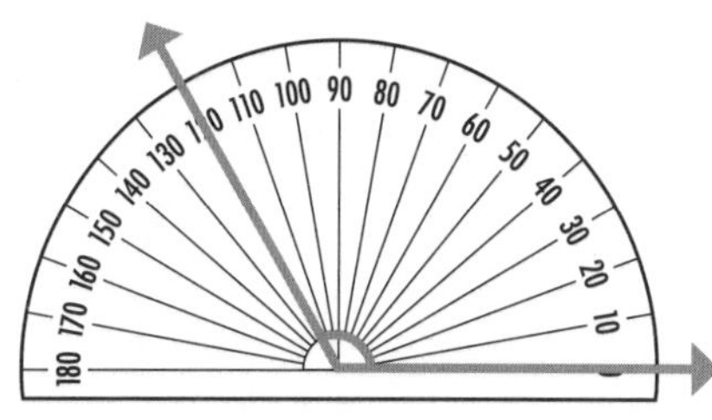

An **obtuse** angle is any angle measuring more than 90°.

WRITE *right*, *acute*, or *obtuse* for each angle.

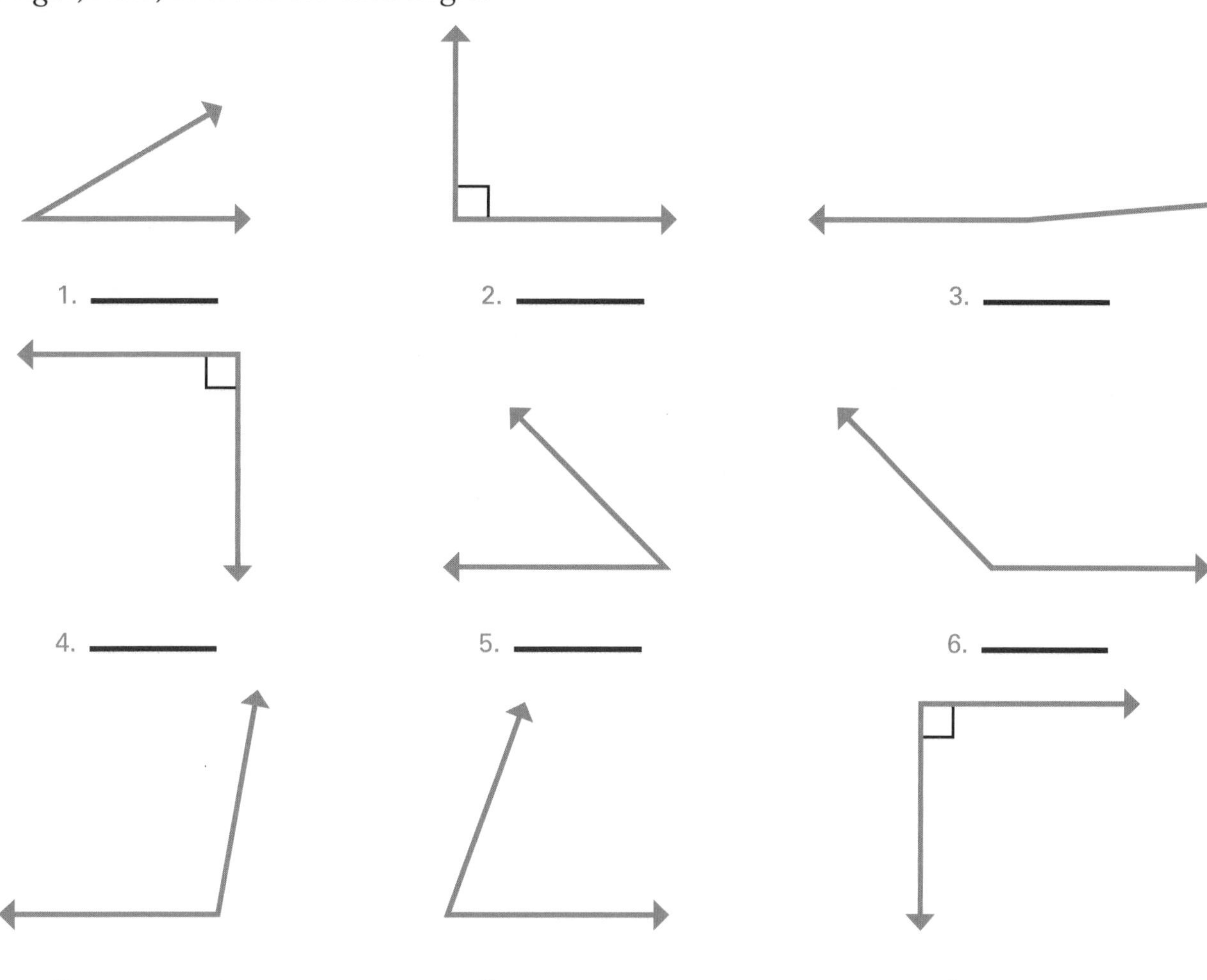

1. ________
2. ________
3. ________
4. ________
5. ________
6. ________
7. ________
8. ________
9. ________

Circle the Same

CIRCLE all of the angles that are in the correct column.

Right	Acute	Obtuse

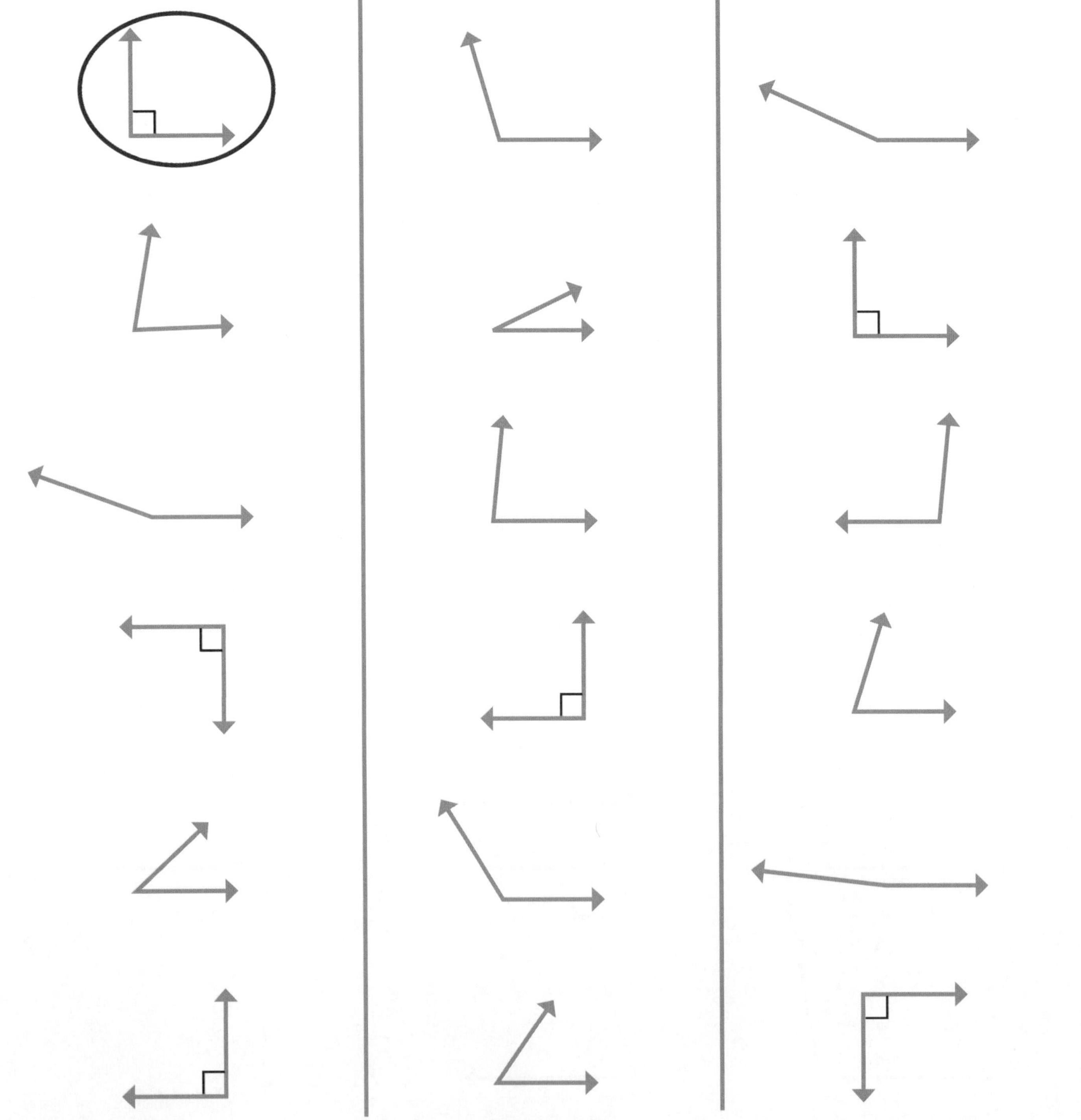

What's My Name?

A **polygon** is a closed plane shape that has three or more sides. Polygons are named according to their number of sides.

A **triangle** has three sides.

A **rectangle** has four sides.

A **square** is a special kind of rectangle that has four equal sides.

A **pentagon** has five sides.

A **hexagon** has six sides.

A **heptagon** has seven sides.

An **octagon** has eight sides.

A **nonagon** has nine sides.

WRITE the name of each polygon.

1. ______________________

2. ______________________

3. ______________________

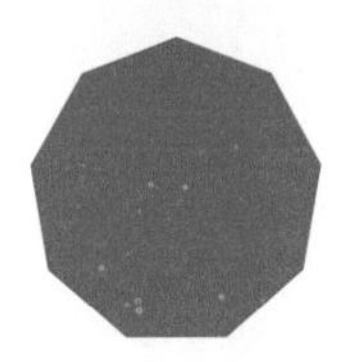

4. ______________________

5. ______________________

6. ______________________

7. ______________________

8. ______________________

Match Up

WRITE number of sides inside each polygon. Then DRAW a line to match each polygon to the correct name.

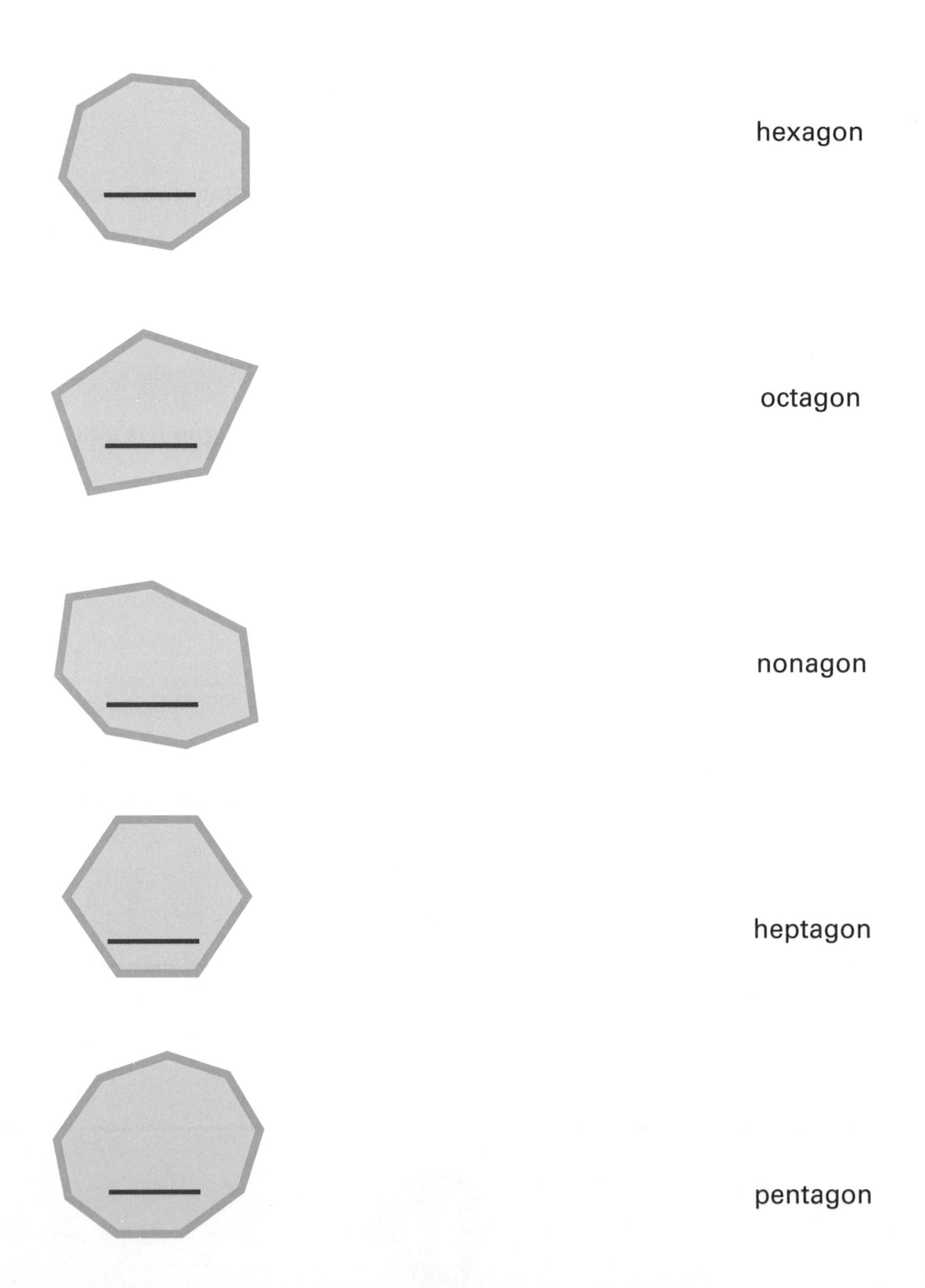

Polygon Pairs

COLOR all of the polygons in each row that match the word.

pentagon

 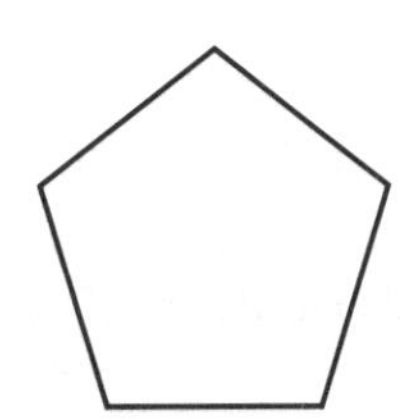 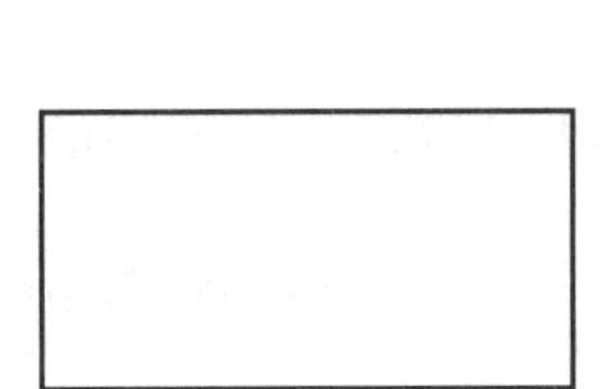 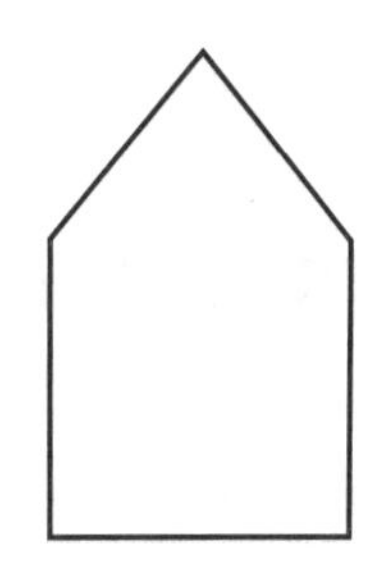

hexagon

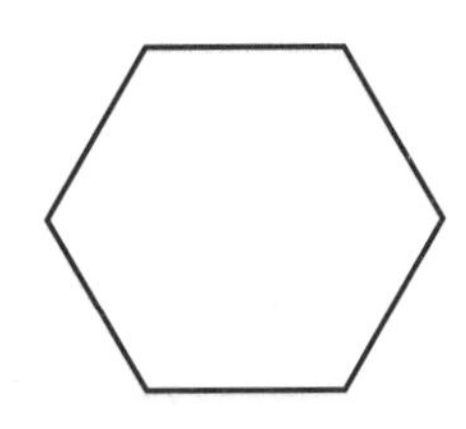 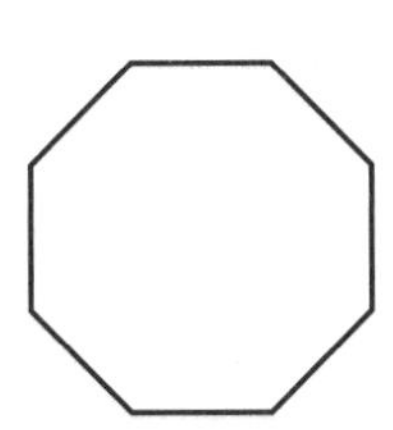 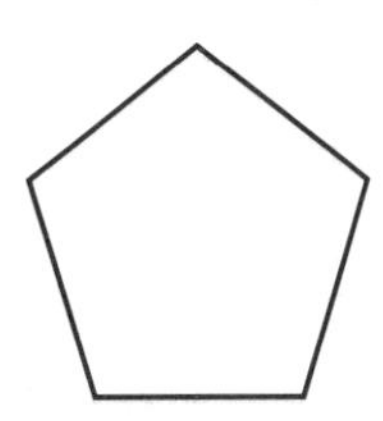 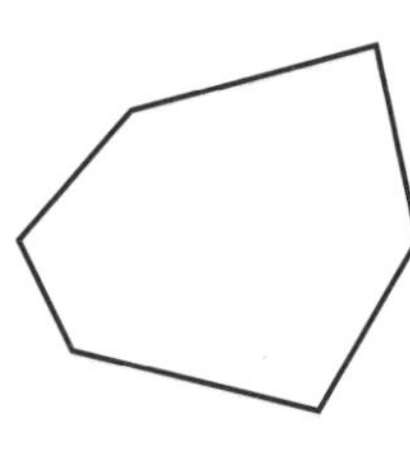

rectangle

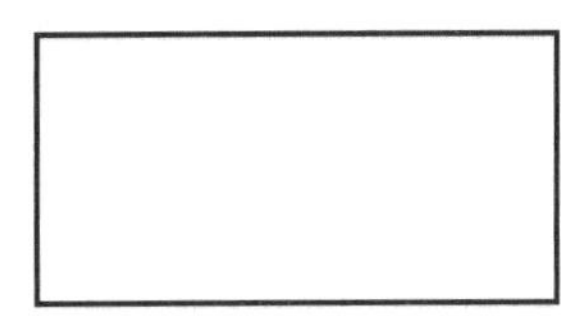 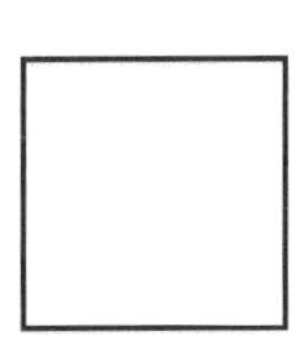 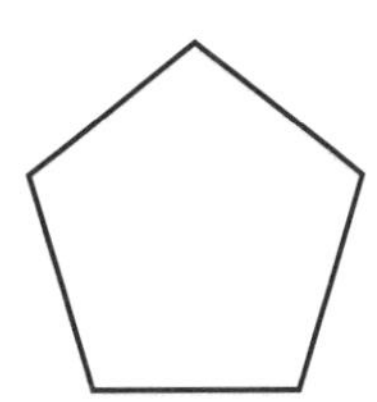 

nonagon

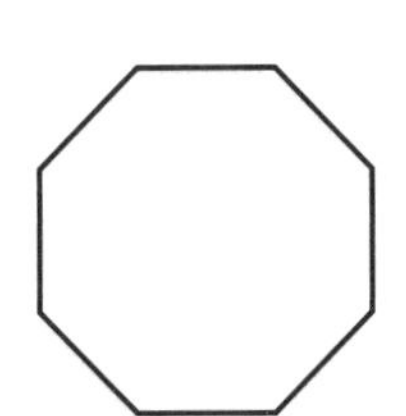  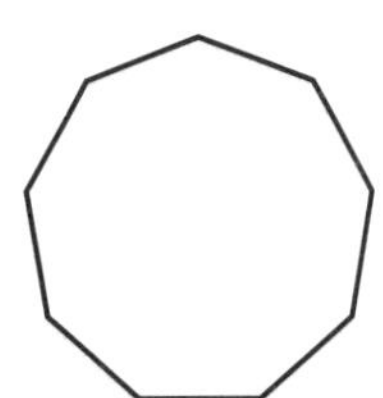 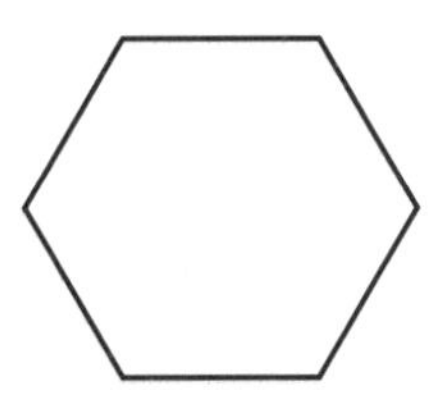

Shape Up

A **vertex** is the point where two sides meet. A triangle has three vertices.

Example:

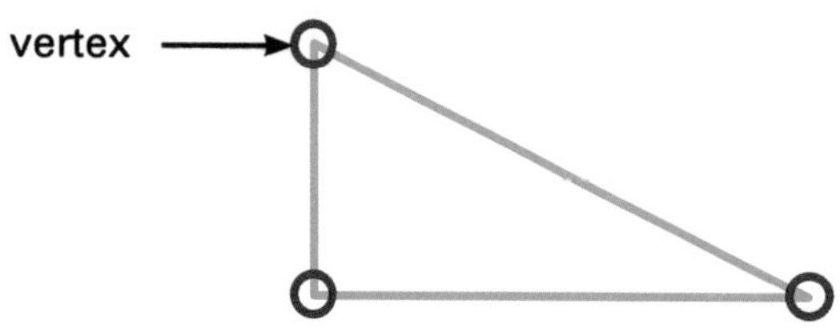

WRITE the name of each shape, the number of sides, and the number of vertices.

	Shape Name	Number of Sides	Number of Vertices

Hidden Angles

Two lines connected by a vertex form an angle. A square has four right angles.

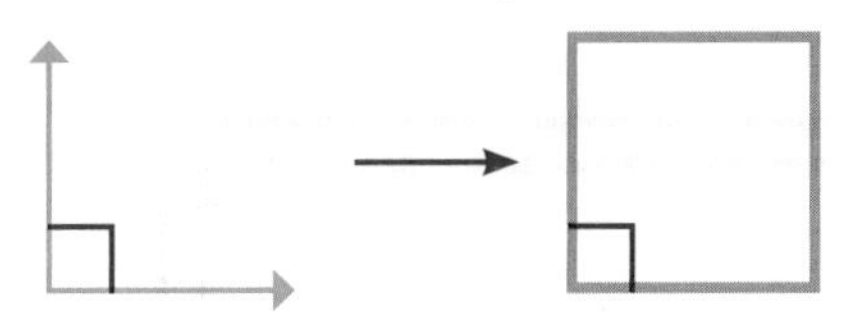

WRITE the number of right, acute, and obtuse angles in each shape.

	Right Angles	Acute Angles	Obtuse Angles
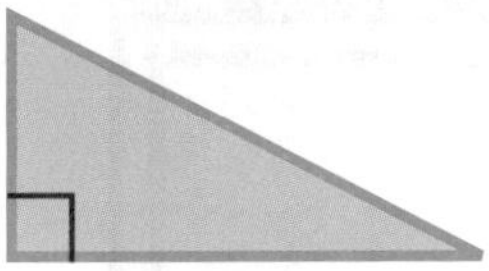			
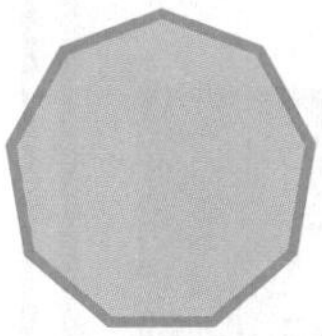			
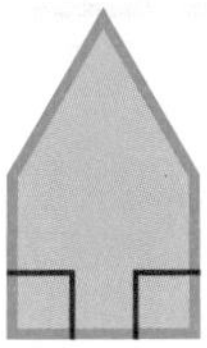			

Mystery Shape

WRITE the number of the mystery shape.

I have no right angles.

I have more vertices than the other shapes in my row.

I have seven sides.

Who am I? ________

Write It

Solid shapes are three-dimensional shapes.

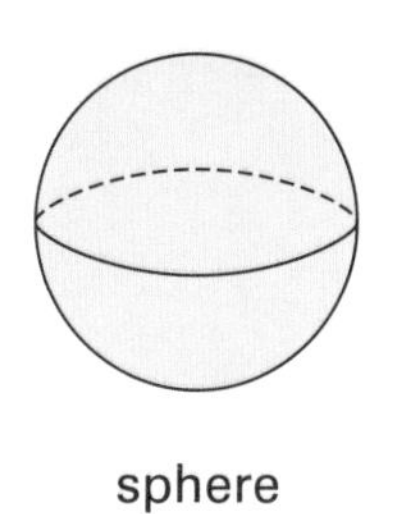

sphere

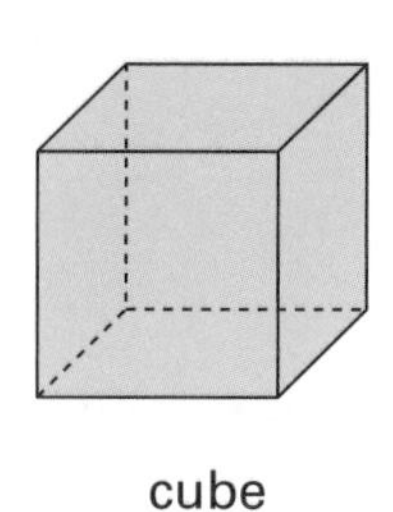

cube

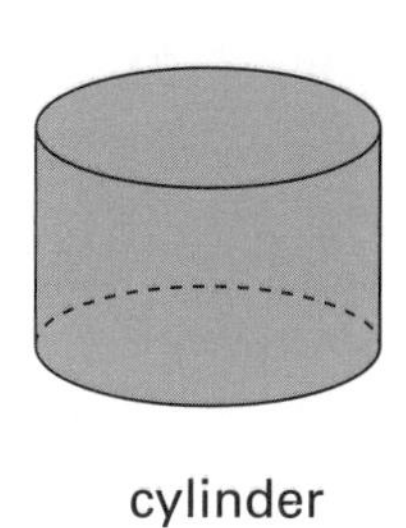

cylinder

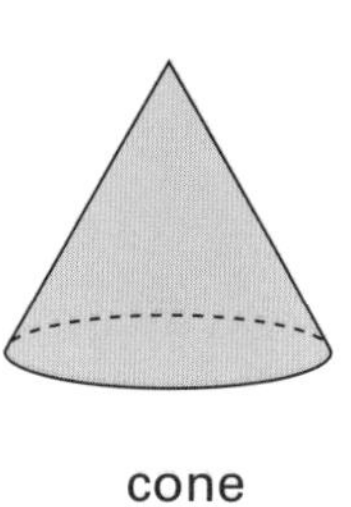

cone

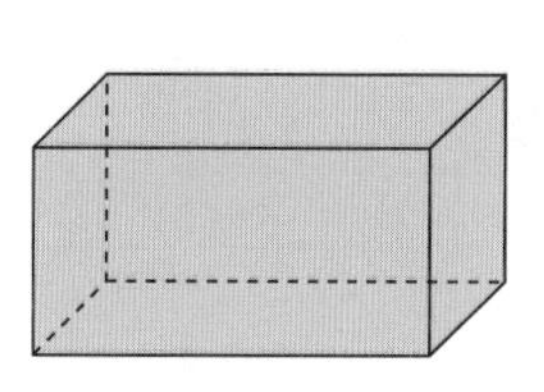

rectangular prism

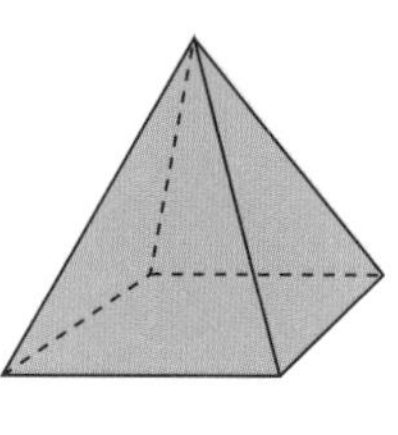

square pyramid

WRITE the name of each shape.

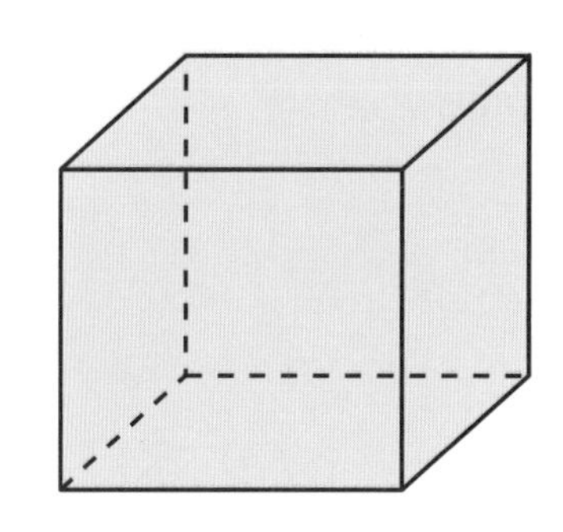

1. ______________________

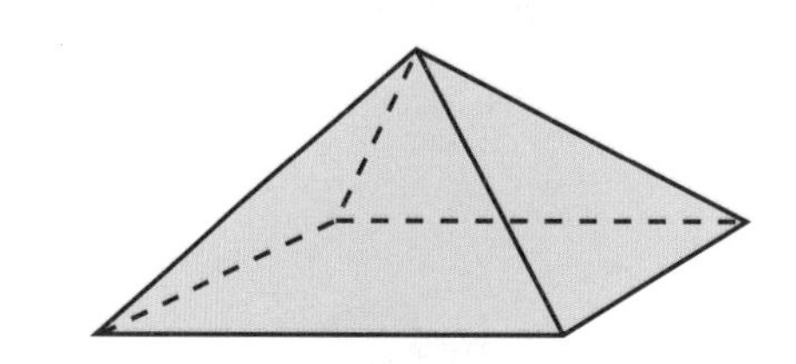

3. ______________________

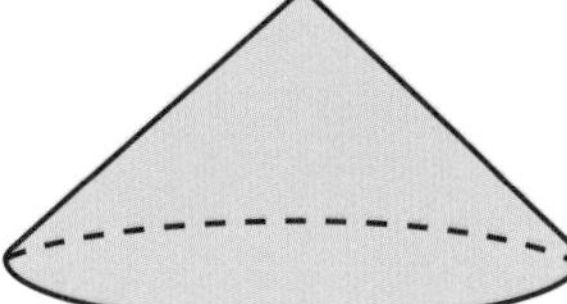

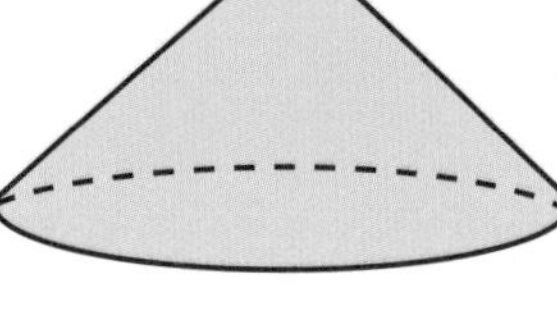

2. ______________________

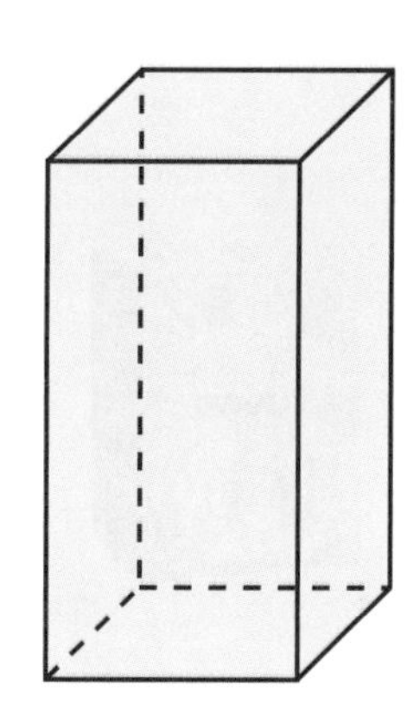

4. ______________________

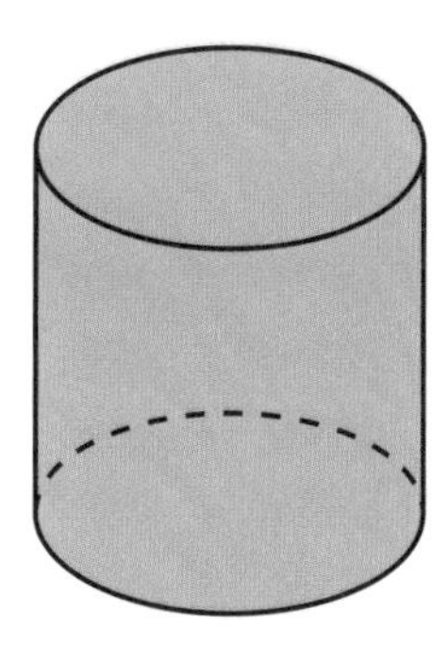

6. ______________________

5. ______________________

Match Up

DRAW a line to match each object with the correct shape name.

rectangular prism

cylinder

cone

cube

sphere

Shape Up

In a three-dimensional shape, a **vertex** is where three or more edges meet. An **edge** is where two sides meet. A **face** is the shape formed by the edges.

Example:

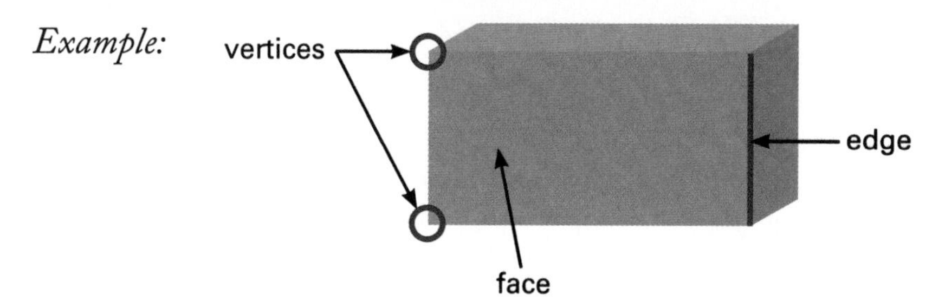

WRITE the name of each shape and the number of vertices, edges, and faces it has.

	Shape Name	Number of Vertices	Number of Edges	Number of Faces
(cube)				
(pyramid)				
(rectangular prism)				

About Face

DRAW all of the shapes that are faces on each three-dimensional shape.

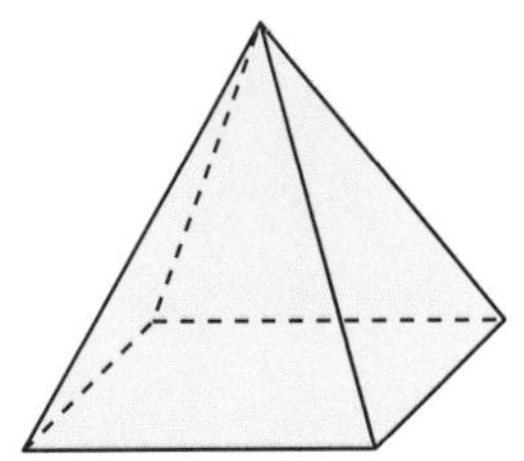

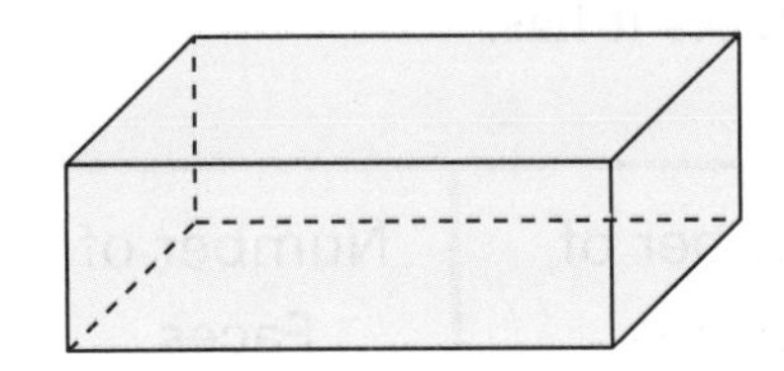

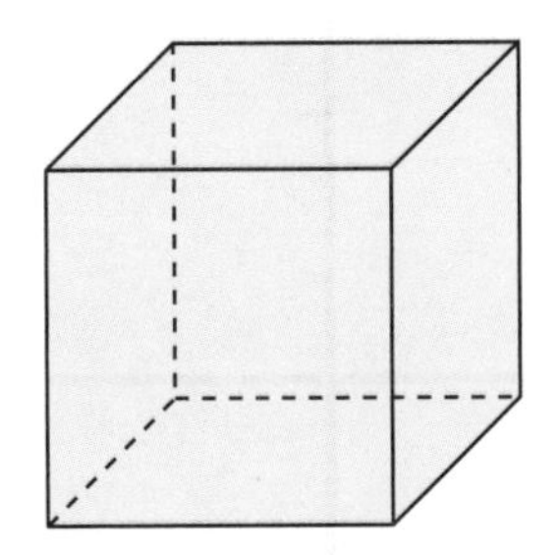

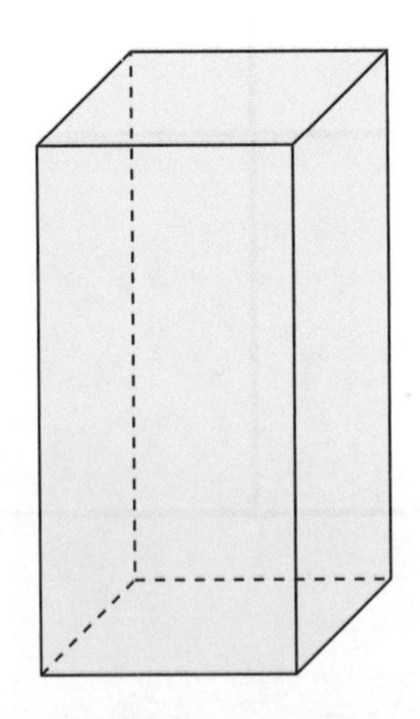

Find the Same

CIRCLE the object in each row that is the same shape as the first shape.

1.

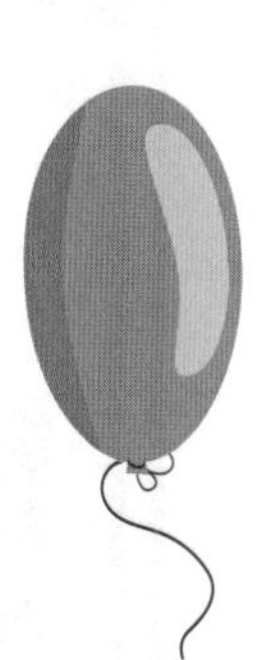

2.

3.

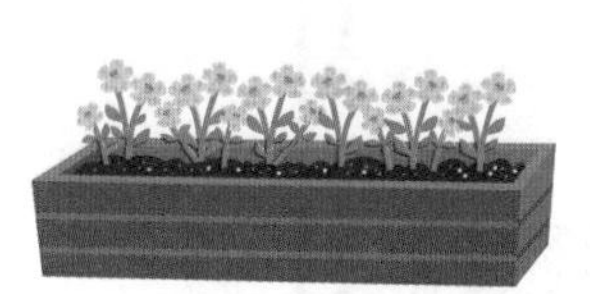
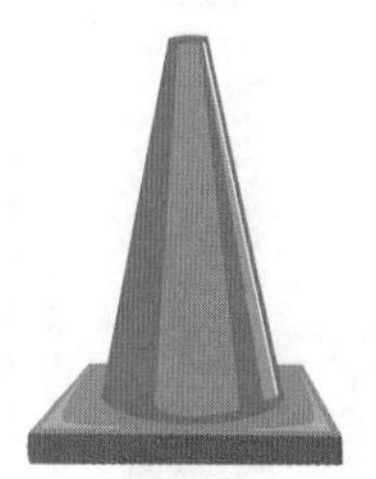

4.

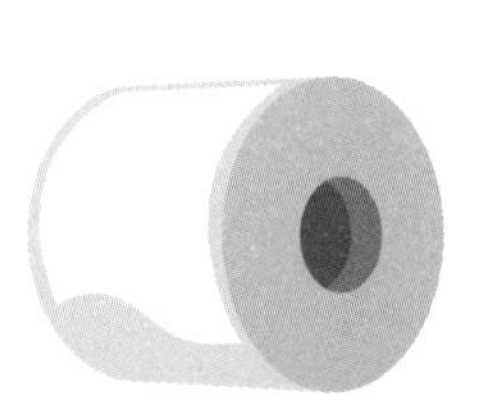

Mystery Shape

WRITE the number of the mystery shape.

At least one of my faces is a square.

I have more than five vertices.

All of my edges are the same length.

Who am I? ________

Circle the Same

Intersecting lines are lines that cross one another.

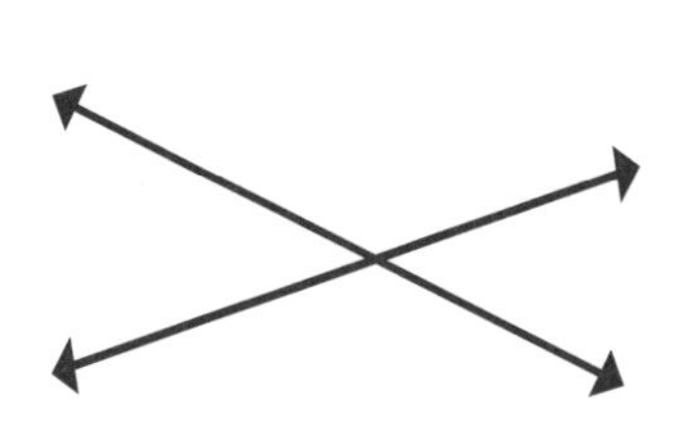

Perpendicular lines intersect to form right angles.

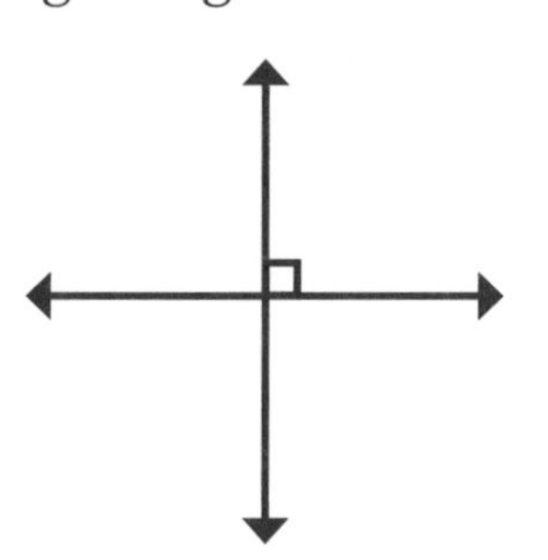

Parallel lines never intersect and are always the same distance apart.

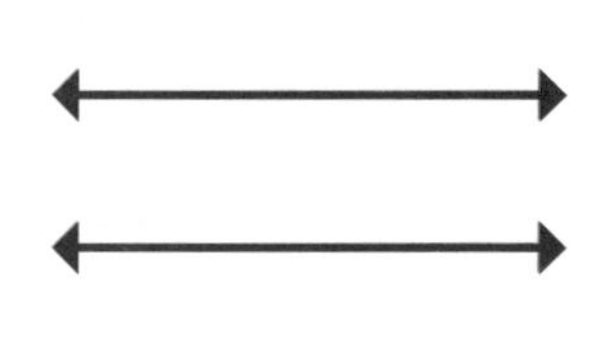

CIRCLE all of the angles that match the word.

Intersecting	Perpendicular	Parallel

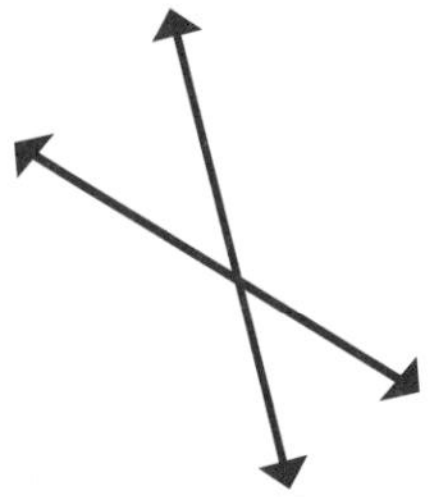

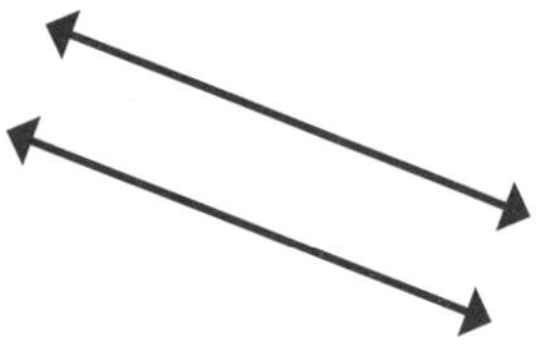

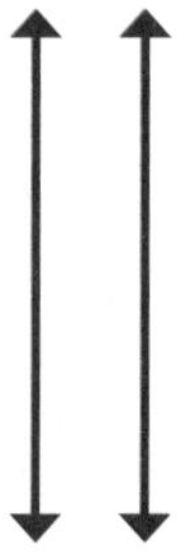

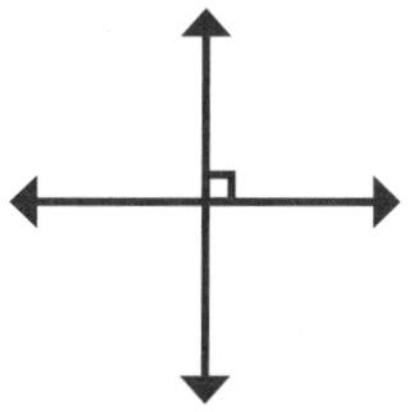

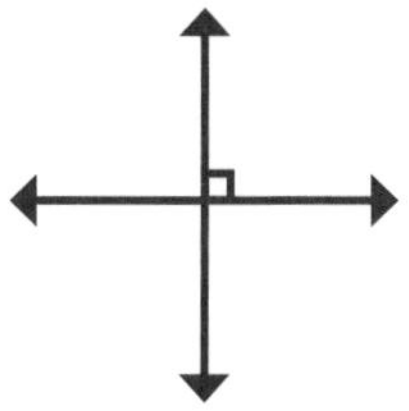

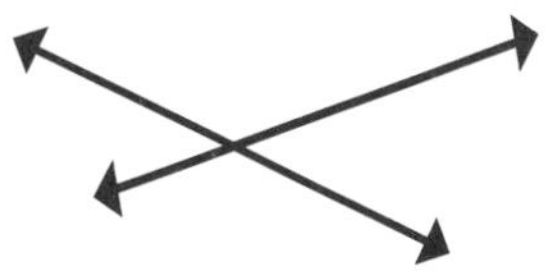

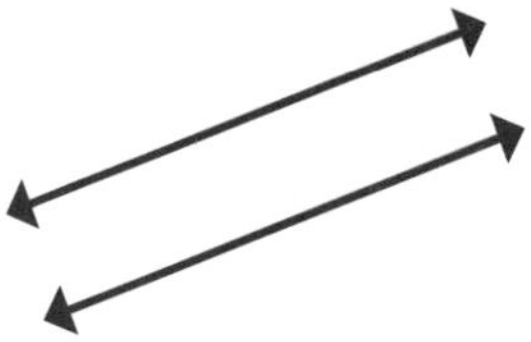

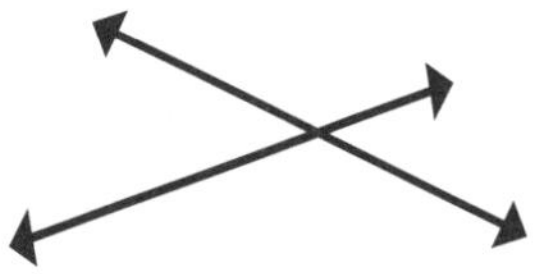

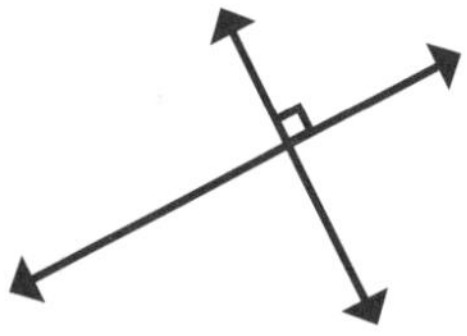

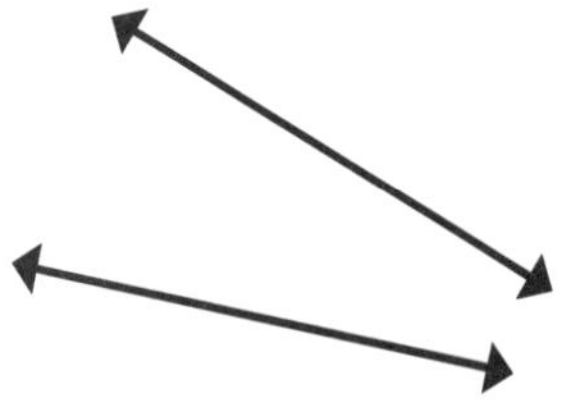

Lines in Shapes

Lines that form shapes can often be perpendicular or parallel.

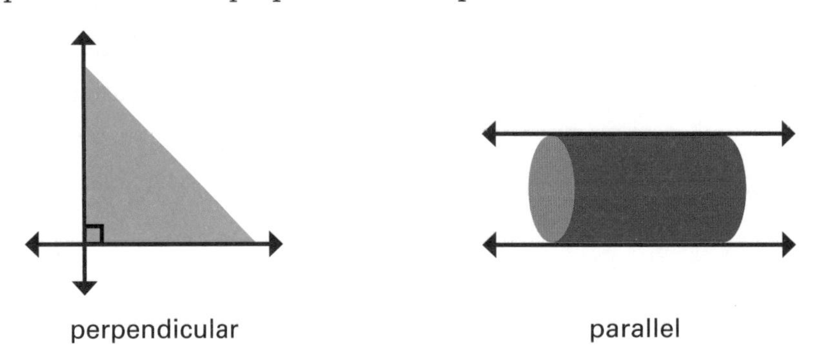

CIRCLE all of the shapes that have at least one pair of perpendicular lines.

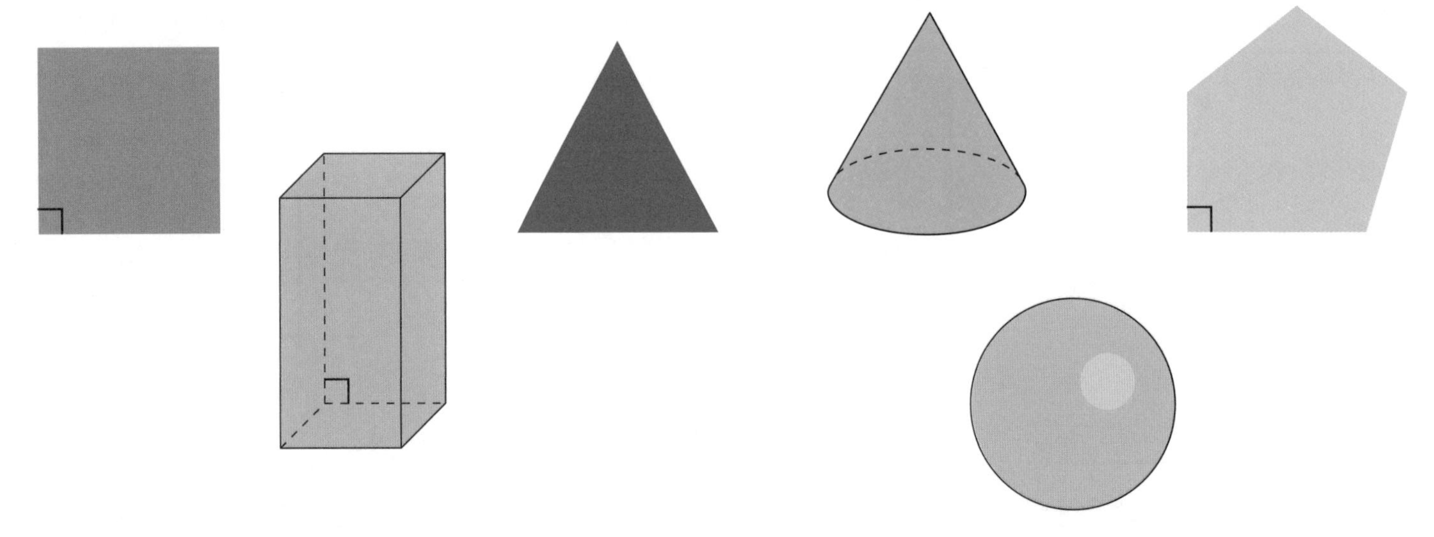

CIRCLE all of the shapes that have at least one pair of parallel lines.

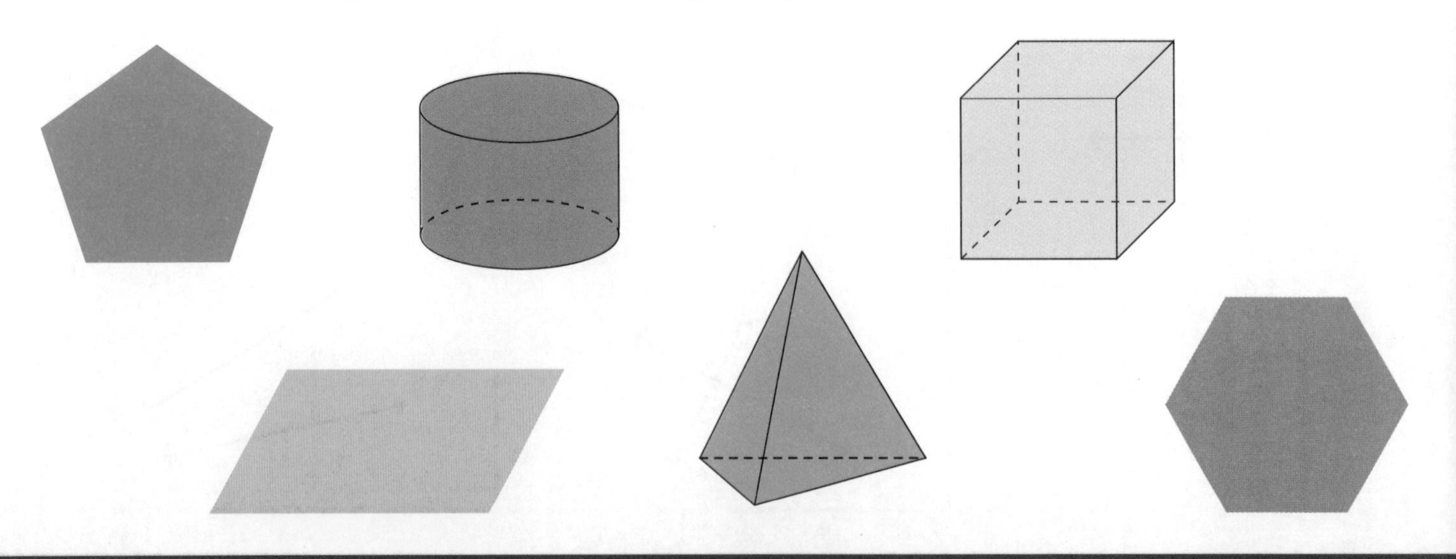

Any Which Way

A **flip**, **slide**, or **turn** has been applied to each shape. WRITE *flip*, *slide*, or *turn* on the line.

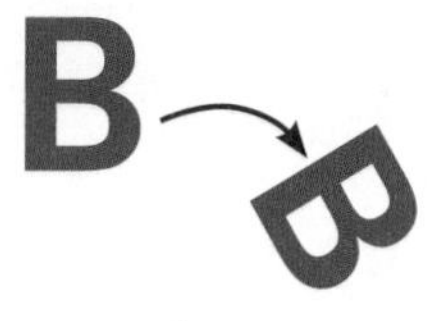

flip slide turn

1. ____________

2. ____________

3. ____________

4. ____________

5. ____________

6. ____________

7. ____________

8. ____________

Perfect Patterns

A **tessellation** is a repeating pattern of shapes that has no gaps or overlapping shapes. DRAW and COLOR the rest of each tessellation.

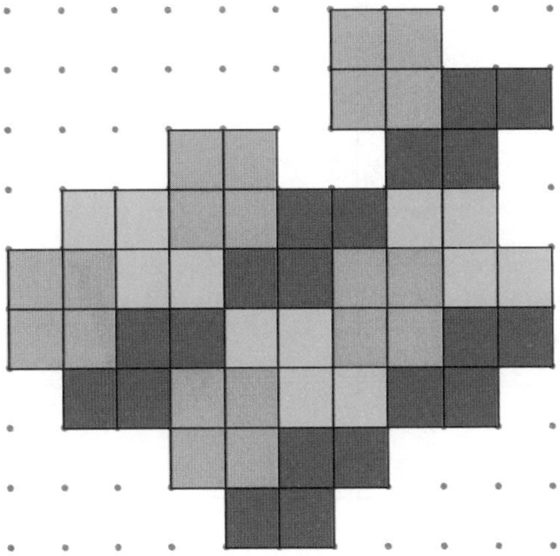

What's My Name?

WRITE the name of each shape.

1. ____________________

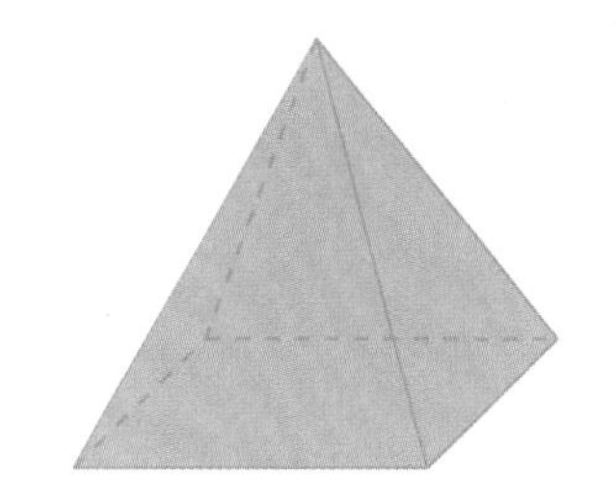

2. ____________________

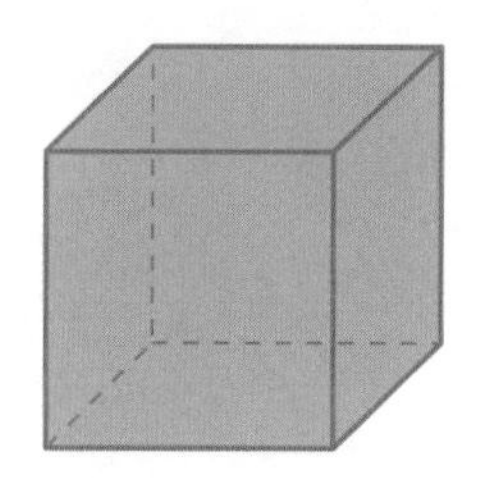

3. ____________________

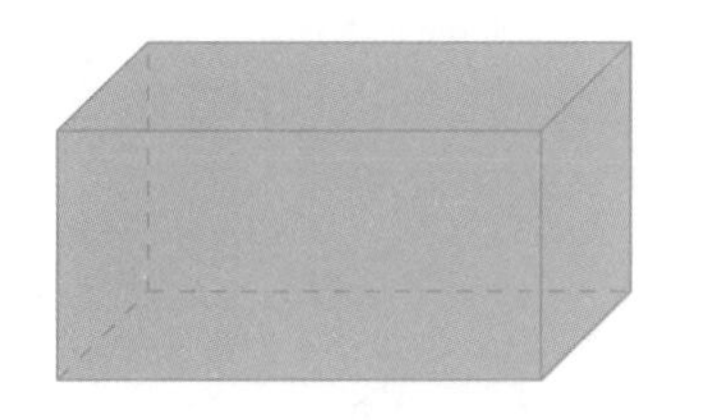

4. ____________________

5. ____________________

6. ____________________

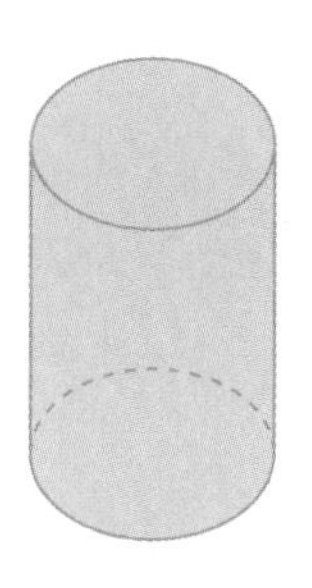

7. ____________________

8. ____________________

9. ____________________

10. ____________________

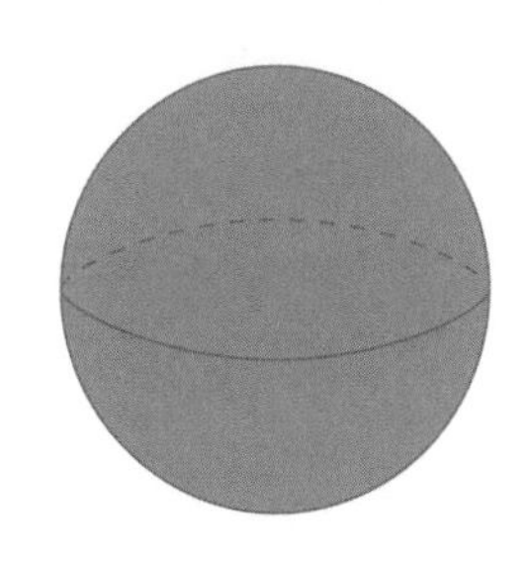

11. ____________________

12. ____________________

Match Up

DRAW a line to match each shape to a description.

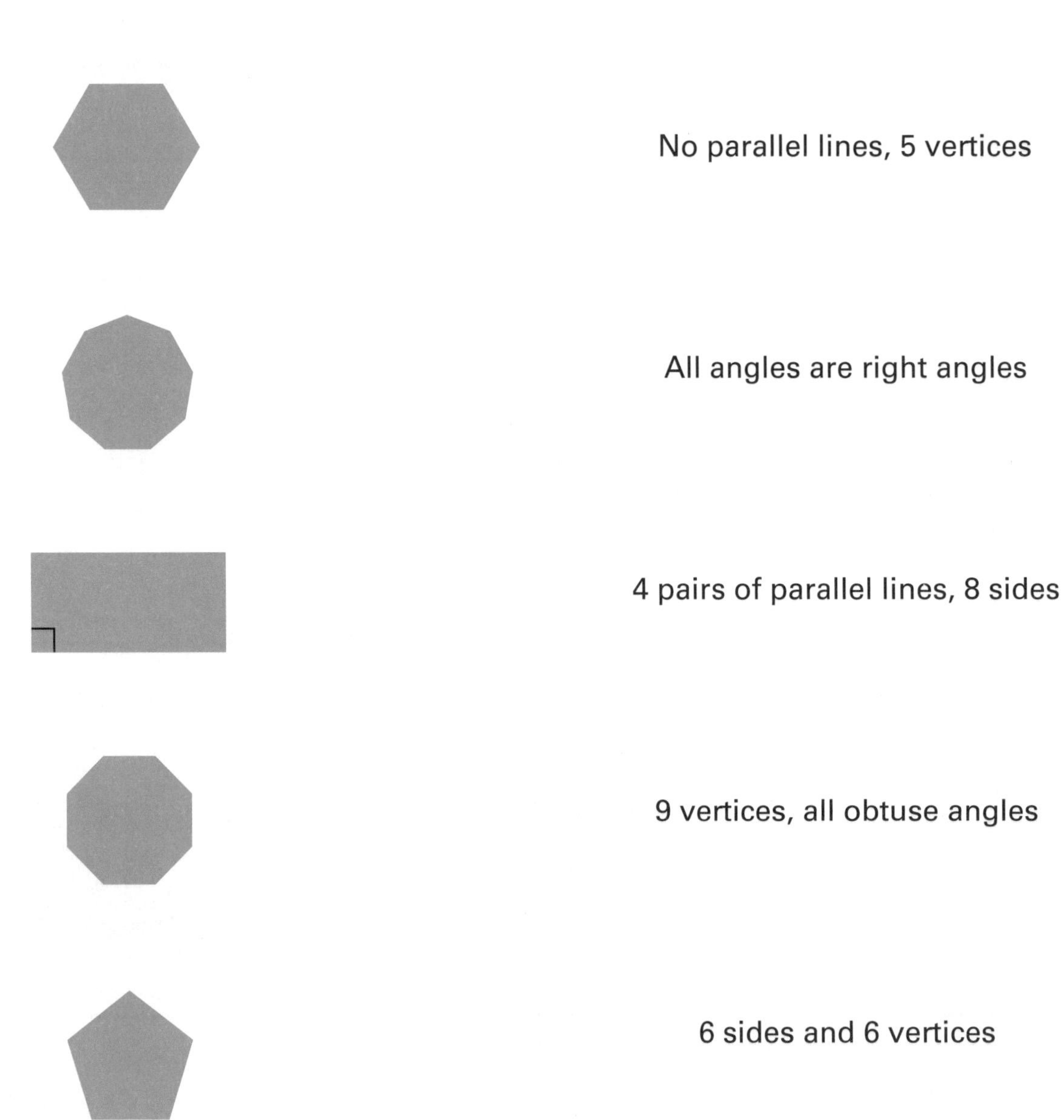

No parallel lines, 5 vertices

All angles are right angles

4 pairs of parallel lines, 8 sides

9 vertices, all obtuse angles

6 sides and 6 vertices

No parallel or perpendicular lines, 7 sides

Match Up

DRAW a line to match each shape to a description.

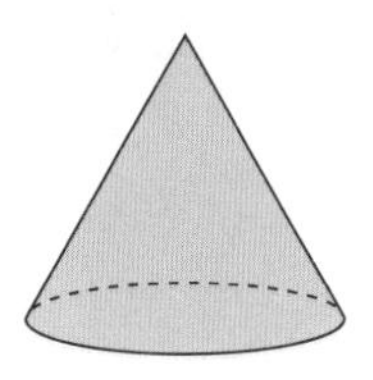

12 edges, 6 faces

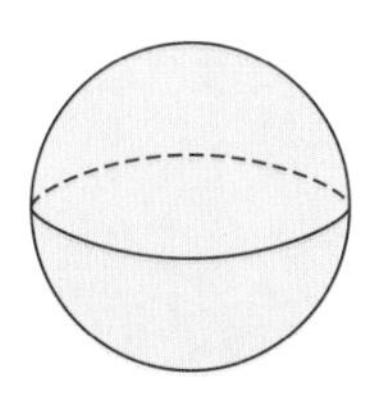

2 faces that are circles

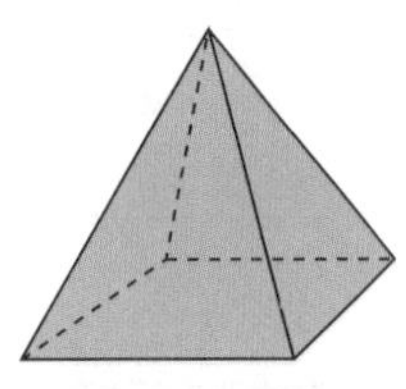

12 edges, all faces the same size

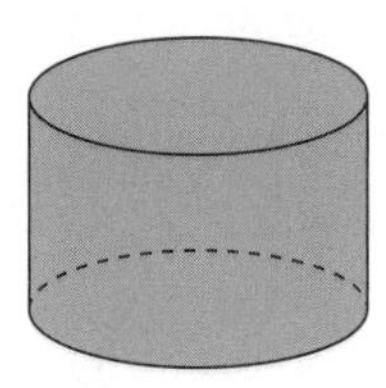

1 face that is a circle

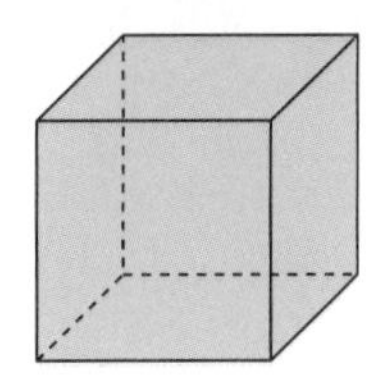

No edges or vertices

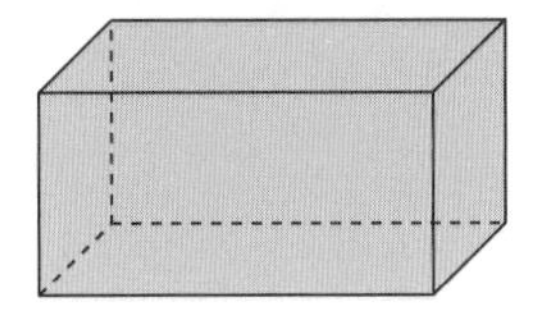

8 edges, 5 vertices

Unit Rewind

WRITE *right*, *acute*, or *obtuse* for each angle.

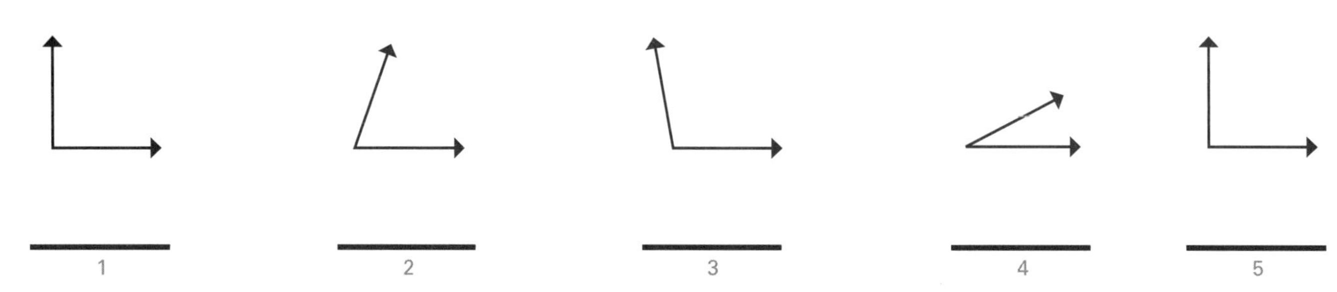

_____ 1

_____ 2

_____ 3

_____ 4

_____ 5

WRITE *parallel*, *perpendicular*, or *intersecting* for each pair of lines.

HINT: Some have more than one correct answer.

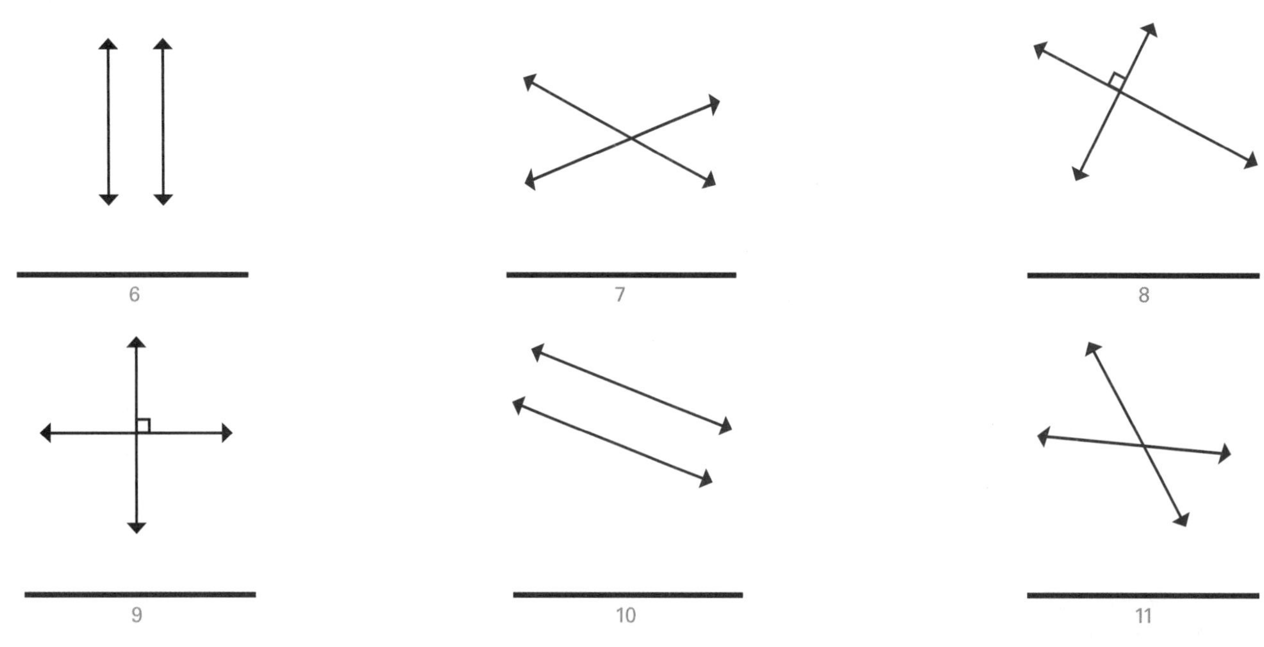

_____ 6

_____ 7

_____ 8

_____ 9

_____ 10

_____ 11

WRITE *flip*, *slide*, or *turn* for each pair of shapes.

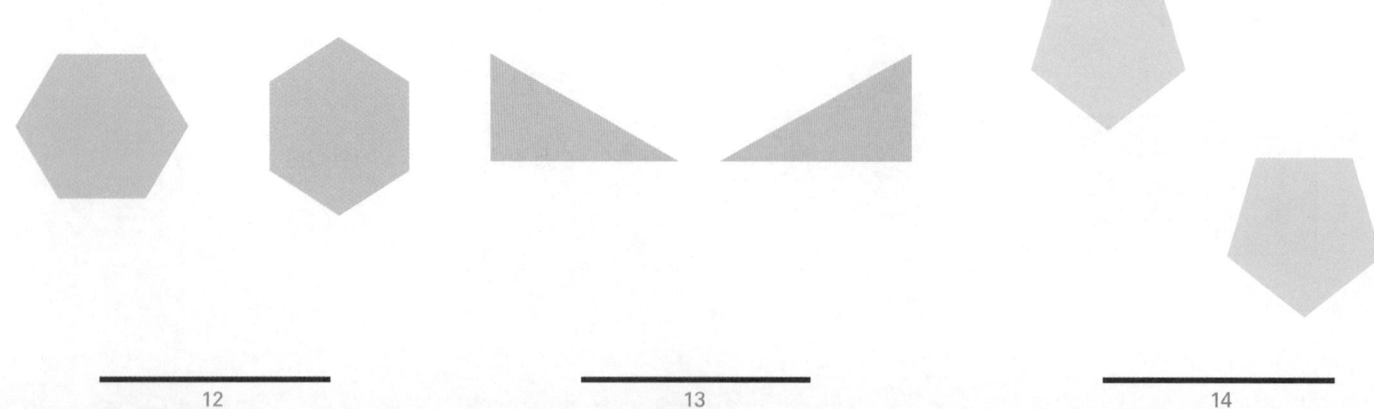

_____ 12

_____ 13

_____ 14

Page 3
1. two thousand, four hundred thirty-nine
2. forty-one thousand, five hundred eighty-two
3. seven hundred thirty-six thousand, one hundred twenty
4. five million, eight hundred twenty-four thousand, four hundred sixteen
5. nine million, three hundred one thousand, five hundred fifty-eight

Page 4
1. 6,942 2. 564,181
3. 2,223,846 4. 90,337
5. 4,119,673 6. 7,314
7. 1,882,450 8. 76,508
9. 230,729 10. 7,491,277

Page 5
1. 8, 5, 2, 3, 7, 6, 2
2. 1, 9, 9, 4, 8, 5, 7
3. 4, 3, 7, 0, 2, 8, 4
4. 6, 2, 5, 1, 3, 1, 9
5. 7, 8, 4, 2, 5, 2, 3
6. 5, 7, 1, 9, 6, 8, 8

Page 6
1. hundred thousands
2. thousands
3. millions
4. tens
5. ten thousands
6. ones
7. hundred thousands
8. hundreds

Page 7
1. > 2. > 3. < 4. <
5. > 6. > 7. > 8. >
9. < 10. < 11. < 12. >
13. > 14. > 15. > 16. <

Page 8
1. < 2. > 3. = 4. >
5. < 6. < 7. = 8. <
9. < 10. > 11. < 12. >
13. < 14. = 15. < 16. >

Page 9
1. 6,874 2. 11,160
3. 28,879 4. 680,391
5. 3,186,797 6. 7,198,003

Page 10
1. 3,420 2. 14,238
3. 45,297 4. 852,268
5. 4,163,588 6. 6,267,828

Page 11
1. 1,000 2. 8,000
3. 6,000 4. 9,000
5. 3,000 6. 5,000
7. 9,000 8. 5,000
9. 5,000 10. 80,000
11. 20,000 12. 20,000
13. 60,000 14. 60,000
15. 70,000 16. 20,000
17. 40,000 18. 30,000

Page 12
1. 700,000 2. 600,000
3. 100,000 4. 400,000
5. 200,000 6. 1,000,000
7. 400,000 8. 600,000
9. 3,000,000 10. 9,000,000
11. 5,000,000 12. 7,000,000
13. 5,000,000 14. 1,000,000
15. 3,000,000 16. 6,000,000

Page 13
Check: 561

Page 14

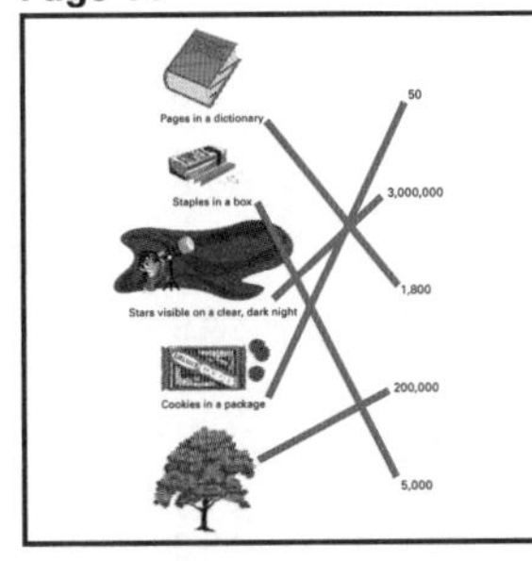

Page 15
1. 682,413
2. 167,521
3. 9,076,803
4. thirty-four thousand, nine hundred eighty-seven
5. four hundred fifty-eight thousand, thirteen
6. five million, three hundred twenty-four thousand, nine hundred ninety-five
7. 3,782,903
8. 5,712,436
9. 1,989,236

Page 16
1. > 2. > 3. < 4. <
5. = 6. >
7. 2,391,000; 5,927,000; 9,466,000
8. 2,390,000; 5,930,000; 9,470,000
9. 2,400,000; 5,900,000; 9,500,000
10. 2,000,000; 6,000,000; 9,000,000
11. 100

Page 17
1. 87,968 2. 17,456
3. 53,955 4. 29,684
5. 58,715 6. 94,597
7. 26,193 8. 79,264
9. 40,236 10. 84,753
11. 65,642 12. 59,695

Page 18
1. 78,583 2. 64,778
3. 90,960 4. 73,091
5. 47,226 6. 99,629
7. 26,038 8. 89,465

Pages 19
1. 50,182 2. 41,409
3. 92,328 4. 76,243
5. 69,021 6. 98,040
7. 33,149 8. 55,331
9. 78,013 10. 89,238
11. 63,082 12. 42,822

Pages 20
1. 14,224 2. 15,105
3. 19,947 4. 18,362
5. 43,979 6. 55,728
7. 65,632 8. 96,099
9. 34,500 10. 86,934
11. 91,536 12. 59,881

Page 21
1. 21,721 2. 53,036
3. 93,433 4. 77,102
5. 13,129 6. 51,213
7. 61,405 8. 43,524
9. 5,328 10. 22,740
11. 14,625 12. 39,351

Page 22
1. 43,587 2. 7,867
3. 57,872 4. 69,609
5. 25,558 6. 48,785
7. 6,347 8. 49,451
9. 75,135 10. 14,783
11. 29,977 12. 23,182

Page 23
1. 37,325 2. 65,529
3. 28,737 4. 43,556
5. 4,815 6. 57,763
7. 25,438 8. 11,936
9. 85,628 10. 27,830
11. 39,669 12. 13,612

Page 24
1. 37,434 2. 62,507
3. 77,128 4. 89,314
5. 88,677 6. 17,636
7. 14,283 8. 51,491
9. 25,849 10. 32,586
11. 11,977 12. 2,013
13. 40,368 14. 30,817
15. 2,392 16. 7,887

Page 25

1. $\begin{array}{r}8{,}576\\+\,1{,}259\\\hline 9{,}835\end{array}\quad\begin{array}{r}8{,}000\\+\,1{,}000\\\hline 9{,}000\end{array}$

2. $\begin{array}{r}9{,}662\\-\,2{,}314\\\hline 7{,}348\end{array}\quad\begin{array}{r}9{,}000\\-\,2{,}000\\\hline 7{,}000\end{array}$

3. $\begin{array}{r}30{,}862\\+\,2{,}775\\\hline 33{,}637\end{array}\quad\begin{array}{r}30{,}000\\+\,2{,}000\\\hline 32{,}000\end{array}$

4. $\begin{array}{r}46{,}237\\-\,4{,}669\\\hline 41{,}568\end{array}\quad\begin{array}{r}40{,}000\\-\,4{,}000\\\hline 36{,}000\end{array}$

5. $\begin{array}{r}40{,}927\\+\,35{,}290\\\hline 76{,}217\end{array}\quad\begin{array}{r}40{,}000\\+\,30{,}000\\\hline 70{,}000\end{array}$

6. $\begin{array}{r}99{,}730\\-\,57{,}594\\\hline 42{,}136\end{array}\quad\begin{array}{r}90{,}000\\-\,50{,}000\\\hline 40{,}000\end{array}$

Page 26

1. $\begin{array}{r}19{,}343\\+\,40{,}489\\\hline 59{,}832\end{array}\quad\begin{array}{r}20{,}000\\+\,40{,}000\\\hline 60{,}000\end{array}$

2. $\begin{array}{r}53{,}677\\-\,24{,}156\\\hline 29{,}521\end{array}\quad\begin{array}{r}50{,}000\\-\,20{,}000\\\hline 30{,}000\end{array}$

3. $\begin{array}{r}65{,}563\\+\,12{,}498\\\hline 78{,}061\end{array}\quad\begin{array}{r}70{,}000\\+\,10{,}000\\\hline 80{,}000\end{array}$

4. $\begin{array}{r}79{,}432\\-\,42{,}722\\\hline 36{,}710\end{array}\quad\begin{array}{r}80{,}000\\-\,40{,}000\\\hline 40{,}000\end{array}$

5. $\begin{array}{r}57{,}249\\+\,28{,}501\\\hline 85{,}750\end{array}\quad\begin{array}{r}60{,}000\\+\,30{,}000\\\hline 90{,}000\end{array}$

6. $\begin{array}{r}64{,}205\\-\,52{,}198\\\hline 12{,}007\end{array}\quad\begin{array}{r}60{,}000\\-\,50{,}000\\\hline 10{,}000\end{array}$

Page 27
1. 91,680 2. 12,326

Page 28

1. $\begin{array}{r}48{,}369\\+\,38{,}848\\\hline 87{,}217\end{array}$

$\begin{array}{r}40{,}000\\+\,30{,}000\\\hline 70{,}000\end{array}\quad\begin{array}{r}50{,}000\\+\,40{,}000\\\hline 90{,}000\end{array}$

2. $\begin{array}{r}20{,}128\\+\,12{,}856\\\hline 32{,}984\end{array}$

$\begin{array}{r}20{,}000\\+\,10{,}000\\\hline 30{,}000\end{array}\quad\begin{array}{r}20{,}000\\+\,10{,}000\\\hline 30{,}000\end{array}$

3. $\begin{array}{r}77{,}807\\-\,54{,}431\\\hline 23{,}376\end{array}$

$\begin{array}{r}70{,}000\\-\,50{,}000\\\hline 20{,}000\end{array}\quad\begin{array}{r}80{,}000\\-\,50{,}000\\\hline 30{,}000\end{array}$

4. $\begin{array}{r}68{,}324\\-\,11{,}584\\\hline 56{,}740\end{array}$

$\begin{array}{r}60{,}000\\-\,10{,}000\\\hline 50{,}000\end{array}\quad\begin{array}{r}70{,}000\\-\,10{,}000\\\hline 60{,}000\end{array}$

Page 29

0	0	0	0	0	0	0	0	0	0	0
0	1	2	3	4	5	6	7	8	9	10
0	2	4	6	8	10	12	14	16	18	20
0	3	6	9	12	15	18	21	24	27	30
0	4	8	12	16	20	24	28	32	36	40
0	5	10	15	20	25	30	35	40	45	50
0	6	12	18	24	30	36	42	48	54	60
0	7	14	21	28	35	42	49	56	63	70
0	8	16	24	32	40	48	56	64	72	80
0	9	18	27	36	45	54	63	72	81	90
0	10	20	30	40	50	60	70	80	90	100

Answers

Page 30

1. 15 2. 72 3. 6
4. 14 5. 30 6. 36
7. 56 8. 0 9. 64
10. 10 11. 63 12. 100
13. 30 14. 3 15. 42
16. 36 17. 80 18. 25
19. 27 20. 0 21. 10
22. 81 23. 24 24. 18
25. 49 26. 20 27. 9
28. 7 29. 48 30. 16

Page 31

1. 424 2. 156 3. 336

Page 32

1. 162 2. 230 3. 434
4. 171 5. 92 6. 280

Page 33

1. 48 2. 79 3. 279
4. 88 5. 39 6. 248
7. 168 8. 186 9. 400
10. 128 11. 219 12. 140
13. 546 14. 126 15. 87
16. 360 17. 208 18. 355

Page 34

1. 114 2. 288 3. 648
4. 210 5. 352 6. 301
7. 208 8. 325 9. 264
10. 48 11. 329 12. 296
13. 306 14. 608 15. 114
16. 212 17. 693 18. 765

Page 35

1. 704 2. 1,752
3. 7,344 4. 852
5. 3,835 6. 2,065
7. 2,421 8. 910
9. 1,328 10. 675
11. 3,598 12. 2,430
13. 2,724 14. 1,126
15. 2,552 16. 1,360
17. 2,784 18. 1,782

Page 36

1. 3,640 2. 744
3. 2,072 4. 3,980
5. 1,134 6. 1,848
7. 4,018 8. 1,161
9. 8,298 10. 2,185

Page 37

1. 1,134 2. 540
3. 2,835 4. 2,220
5. 3,528 6. 4,928
7. 4,230 8. 625
9. 1,001 10. 6,324
11. 779 12. 2,688
13. 8,772 14. 18,428
15. 54,600 16. 14,952
17. 10,665 18. 79,622

Page 38

1. 884 2. 3,150
3. 1,887 4. 4,416
5. 1,088 6. 5,740
7. 4,169 8. 12,685
9. 48,716 10. 52,101

Page 39

5: 5, 1, 7, 4, 10, 3, 2, 6, 9, 8
3: 5, 9, 4, 1, 10, 6, 2, 8, 3, 7
8: 1, 6, 10, 5, 2, 3, 7, 9, 4, 8
4: 6, 10, 4, 5, 8, 2, 3, 7, 9, 1
7: 3, 9, 4, 8, 5, 10, 2, 1, 7, 6
9: 2, 10, 1, 6, 7, 3, 4, 8, 9, 5

Page 40

1. 2 2. 7 3. 10
4. 9 5. 9 6. 7
7. 8 8. 8 9. 9
10. 1 11. 3 12. 8
13. 9 14. 10 15. 5
16. 9 17. 5 18. 2
19. 7 20. 10 21. 8
22. 4 23. 1 24. 3
25. 4 26. 10 27. 4
28. 5 29. 5 30. 8
31. 8 32. 9

Page 41

1. 11 2. 12 3. 16
4. 4 5. 14

Page 42

1. 18 2. 21 3. 12
4. 21 5. 24 6. 11
7. 13 8. 46 9. 17
10. 32 11. 25 12. 27
13. 34 14. 13 15. 12
16. 11 17. 12 18. 49

Page 43

1. 29 2. 52 3. 62
4. 99 5. 34 6. 63
7. 35 8. 41 9. 83
10. 96 11. 81 12. 80
13. 78 14. 57 15. 124

Page 44

1. 14
84 ÷ 6 = 14
84 ÷ 14 = 6
6 x 14 = 84
14 x 6 = 84

2. 28
56 ÷ 2 = 28
56 ÷ 28 = 2
2 x 28 = 56
28 x 2 = 56

3. 66
594 ÷ 9 = 66
594 ÷ 66 = 9
9 x 66 = 594
66 x 9 = 594

4. 59
413 ÷ 7 = 59
413 ÷ 59 = 7
7 x 59 = 413
59 x 7 = 413

5. 187
748 ÷ 4 = 187
748 ÷ 187 = 4
4 x 187 = 748
187 x 4 = 748

Page 44 (continued)

6. 272
816 ÷ 3 = 272
816 ÷ 272 = 3
3 x 272 = 816
272 x 3 = 816

Page 45

1. 3 2. 3 3. 5
4. 6 5. 7 6. 12
7. 20 8. 16 9. 39
10. 15 11. 31 12. 13
13. 52 14. 21 15. 25

Page 46

1. $22\overline{)616}$ = 28; $28 \times 22 = 616$
2. $64\overline{)704}$ = 11; $11 \times 64 = 704$
3. $12\overline{)432}$ = 36; $36 \times 12 = 432$
4. $30\overline{)630}$ = 21; $21 \times 30 = 630$
5. $34\overline{)510}$ = 15; $15 \times 34 = 510$
6. $14\overline{)728}$ = 52; $52 \times 14 = 728$

Page 47

1. 525, 84, 210
2. 1,116

Page 48

1. 68 2. 153
3. 325 4. 144
5. 328 6. 282
7. 853 8. 4,608
9. 894 10. 2,835
11. 3,910 12. 7,560
13. 996 14. 1,480
15. 3,416 16. 4,158
17. 1,971 18. 702
19. 15,456 20. 12,240
21. 33,957 22. 34,776
23. 29,632 24. 55,860

Page 49

1. 180, 108, 36
2. 52

Page 50

1. 15 2. 28 3. 11
4. 6 5. 5 6. 38
7. 99 8. 127 9. 65
10. 22

11. 20 ÷ 4 = 5
20 ÷ 5 = 4
4 x 5 = 20
5 x 4 = 20

Page 50 (continued)

12. 78 ÷ 6 = 13
78 ÷ 13 = 6
6 x 13 = 78
13 x 6 = 78

13. 736 ÷ 23 = 32
736 ÷ 32 = 23
23 x 32 = 736
32 x 23 = 736

Page 51

1. $\frac{3}{4}$ 2. $\frac{5}{10}$ 3. $\frac{5}{6}$
4. $\frac{1}{4}$ 5. $\frac{4}{7}$ 6. $\frac{7}{12}$

Page 52

$\frac{1}{3}$ $\frac{4}{5}$
$\frac{8}{11}$ $\frac{2}{6}$
$\frac{5}{9}$ $\frac{3}{8}$

Page 53

$\frac{3}{4}$ (circled) $\frac{2}{5}$
$\frac{1}{6}$ $\frac{1}{3}$ (circled)
$\frac{2}{3}$ (circled) $\frac{4}{8}$
$\frac{5}{6}$ $\frac{6}{7}$ (circled)
$\frac{7}{12}$ $\frac{7}{9}$ (circled)

Page 54

1. > 2. < 3. < 4. >
5. > 6. = 7. > 8. <
9. > 10. < 11. < 12. >
13. > 14. < 15. = 16. >

Page 55

1. $\frac{3}{4}$ 2. $\frac{7}{9}$ 3. $\frac{10}{8}$
4. $\frac{7}{7}$ 5. $\frac{7}{5}$ 6. $\frac{5}{6}$

Page 56

1. $\frac{5}{6}$ 2. $\frac{5}{3}$ (circled) 3. $\frac{8}{10}$
4. $\frac{10}{9}$ (circled) 5. $\frac{4}{7}$ 6. $\frac{7}{5}$ (circled)
7. $\frac{3}{4}$ 8. $\frac{4}{2}$ (circled) 9. $\frac{16}{12}$ (circled)
10. $\frac{5}{6}$ 11. $\frac{13}{11}$ (circled) 12. $\frac{8}{8}$

Page 57

1. $\frac{2}{4}$ 2. $\frac{5}{8}$ 3. $\frac{1}{6}$
4. $\frac{3}{5}$ 5. $\frac{6}{12}$ 6. $\frac{3}{7}$

Page 58

1. $\frac{1}{6}$ 2. $\frac{2}{8}$ 3. $\frac{1}{5}$
4. $\frac{3}{10}$ 5. $\frac{3}{12}$ 6. $\frac{2}{7}$
7. $\frac{4}{9}$ 8. $\frac{2}{4}$ 9. $\frac{6}{8}$
10. $\frac{4}{5}$ 11. $\frac{4}{10}$ 12. $\frac{6}{6}$

Page 59

1. $\frac{3}{10}$, 0.3 2. $\frac{6}{10}$, 0.6
3. $\frac{7}{10}$, 0.7 4. $\frac{1}{10}$, 0.1
5. $\frac{9}{10}$, 0.9 6. $\frac{5}{10}$, 0.5

Page 60

1. $\frac{76}{100}$, 0.76 2. $\frac{12}{100}$, 0.12
3. $\frac{41}{100}$, 0.41 4. $\frac{99}{100}$, 0.99

Page 61

1. 1.48 2. 3.77 3. 5.67
4. 0.86 5. 7.09

Page 62

1. 0.5, 0.6, 0.7, 0.8, 0.9
2. 2.1, 2.3, 2.5, 2.8, 3.0
3. 5.0, 5.1, 5.2, 5.4, 5.6, 5.7, 5.9
4. 9.1, 9.2, 9.3, 9.4, 9.5, 9.6, 9.7, 9.8, 9.9
5. 3.5, 3.7, 3.8, 4.0, 4.2
6. 7.8, 8.0, 8.1, 8.3, 8.4, 8.5, 8.7, 8.8

Page 63

0.5	0.3
0.2	0.8
0.9	0.7
0.68	0.93
0.46	0.42

Page 64

1. < 2. > 3. < 4. <
5. > 6. < 7. = 8. >
9. > 10. = 11. < 12. >
13. < 14. < 15. < 16. =
17. < 18. > 19. > 20. >

Page 65

1. 17.83 2. 27.79
3. 46.93 4. 39.73
5. 52.97 6. 68.38
7. 865.75 8. 187.94
9. 785.52 10. 568.19
11. 642.28 12. 996.45

Page 66

1. 15.31 2. 60.20
3. 71.36 4. 11.03
5. 3.12 6. 40.70
7. 331.60 8. 521.21
9. 434.13 10. 163.22
11. 605.67 12. 51.30

Page 67

1. 8.4 2. 12.50
3. 90.77 4. 128.11
5. 71.62 6. 115.61
7. 646.93 8. 507.44
9. 290.39 10. 622.36
11. 897.21 12. 480.25

Page 68

1. 2.9 2. 3.56
3. 29.28 4. 40.7
5. 18.92 6. 15.88
7. 770.67 8. 39.26
9. 228.51 10. 559.45
11. 91.18 12. 362.86

Page 69

1. $\frac{1}{3}$ 2. $\frac{4}{9}$ 3. $\frac{5}{6}$
4. 0.7 5. 0.2 6. 0.36
7. 0.82

Page 70

1. Dante, Rachel, Nora
2. $\frac{8}{10}$ 3. $\frac{4}{10}$
4. $31.82

Page 71

1. = 2. > 3. < 4. >
5. < 6. = 7. > 8. <
9. $\frac{5}{6}$ 10. $\frac{4}{7}$ 11. $\frac{6}{5}$
12. $\frac{2}{4}$ 13. $\frac{11}{10}$ 14. $\frac{3}{3}$
15. $\frac{4}{9}$ 16. $\frac{2}{5}$ 17. $\frac{3}{8}$
18. $\frac{5}{10}$ 19. $\frac{4}{7}$ 20. $\frac{1}{12}$

Page 72

1. < 2. = 3. >
4. > 5. > 6. <
7. = 8. < 9. 1.8
10. 4.6 11. 7.33 12. 76.91
13. 186.12 14. 664.52
15. 1.5 16. 5.3
17. 3.71 18. 28.05
19. 426.71 20. 293.00

Page 73

1. 2.3 2. 8.6 3. 5.6
4. 6.4 5. 15.6

Page 74

1. km 2. m 3. cm
4. mm 5. m 6. km
7. m 8. cm

Page 75

1. 600 2. 120 3. 10,000
4. 3 5. 25 6. 250
7. 6 8. 4,600 9. 9
10. 0.5 11. 0.8 12. 500

Page 76

1. 1 km 2. 2 m
3. 200 cm 4. 40 m
5. 2,500 m 6. 6,000 mm

Page 77

1. $1\frac{3}{4}$ 2. $3\frac{1}{2}$ 3. $\frac{3}{4}$
4. $2\frac{1}{4}$ 5. $6\frac{3}{4}$

Page 78

1. in. 2. yd
3. ft 4. mi
5. in. 6. yd
7. mi 8. ft

Page 79

1. 24 2. 3 3. 36
4. 5,280 5. 72 6. 2
7. 624 8. 10,560 9. 28
10. 2 11. $\frac{1}{2}$ 12. $\frac{1}{3}$

Page 80

1. 1 in. 2. 2 ft 3. 40 in.
4. 1,729 yd 5. 180 in. 6. 120 ft

Page 81

1. 12, 8 2. 16, 8
3. 16, 10 4. 20, 12

Page 82

1. 80 2. 58
3. 108 4. 96

Page 83

1. 150 2. 456
3. 1,656 4. 256

Page 84

1. 24, 32 2. 28, 49
3. 28, 45

Page 85

1. T 2. lb 3. oz 4. T
5. oz 6. lb 7. T 8. oz

Page 86

1. 2,336 2. 3,600
3. 848 4. 1,152

Page 87

1. 2. 2. 2.
3. 224 4. 8,000
5. 800 6. 12
7. 10 8. 12,000
9. 1,600 10. 1,000
11. 4 12. 8

Page 88

Page 89

1. g 2. kg 3. mg 4. g
5. kg 6. mg 7. g 8. g

Page 90

1. 1,100 2. 200
3. 600 4. 9,000

Page 91

1. 2,000 2. 6 3. 2
4. 100 5. 12,000 6. 10
7. 5 8. 500 9. 0.6
10. 0.4 11. 0.1 12. 2,300

Page 92

Page 93

1. 6.7 2. 4.5 3. 8.2
4. $2\frac{1}{2}$ 5. $4\frac{3}{4}$ 6. $3\frac{1}{4}$

Page 94

1. 20, 15 2. 12, 9
3. 42, 98 4. 14, 10

Page 95

1. gram 2. foot
3. ton 4. inch
5. mile 6. milligram
7. kilogram 8. centimeter

Page 96

1. 384 2. 240
3. 15,000 4. 9
5. 4 6. 12
7. 50 8. 880
9. 700 10. 5
11. 6 12. 2
13. 10,000
14. $\frac{1}{4}$ or 0.25
15. $1\frac{1}{2}$ or 1.5

Answers

Page 97

1. acute 2. right 3. obtuse
4. right 5. acute 6. obtuse
7. obtuse 8. acute 9. right

Page 98

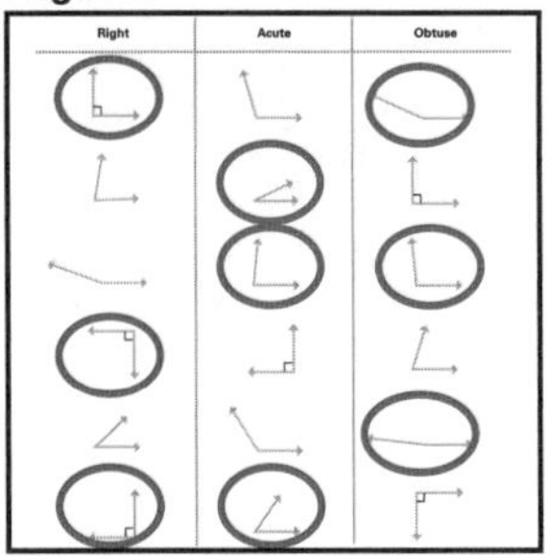

Page 99

1. pentagon
2. heptagon
3. square or rectangle
4. nonagon
5. octagon
6. triangle
7. rectangle
8. hexagon

Page 100

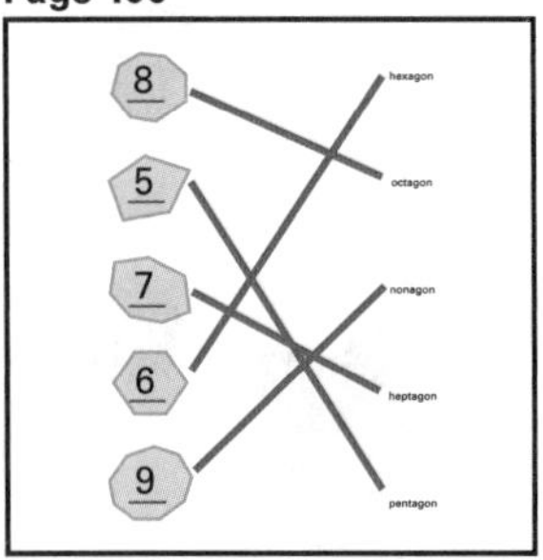

Page 101

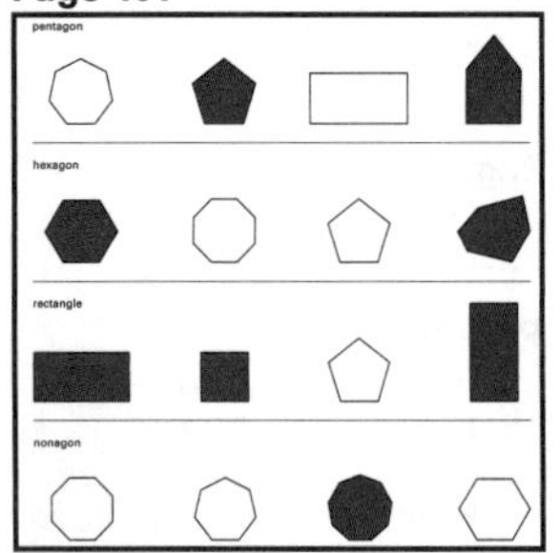

Page 102

pentagon	5	5
nonagon	9	9
rectangle	4	4
heptagon	7	7
hexagon	6	6
octagon	8	8

Page 103

4	0	0
0	2	2
1	2	0
0	0	9
2	1	2
0	3	0

Page 104

7

Page 105

1. cube
2. cone
3. square pyramid
4. sphere
5. cylinder
6. rectangular prism

Page 106

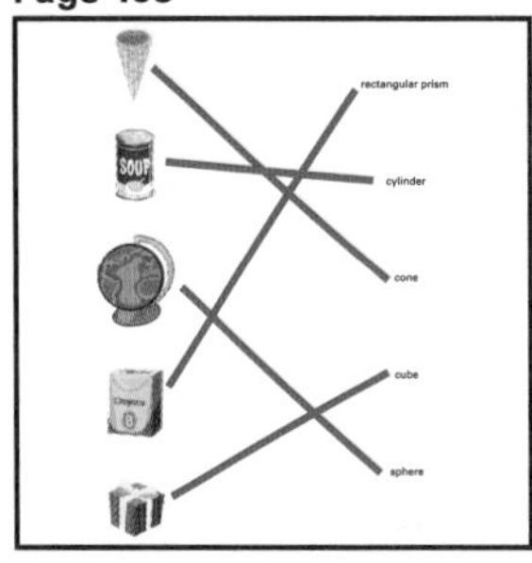

Page 107

cube	8	12	6
square pyramid	5	8	5
rectangular prism	8	12	6

Page 108

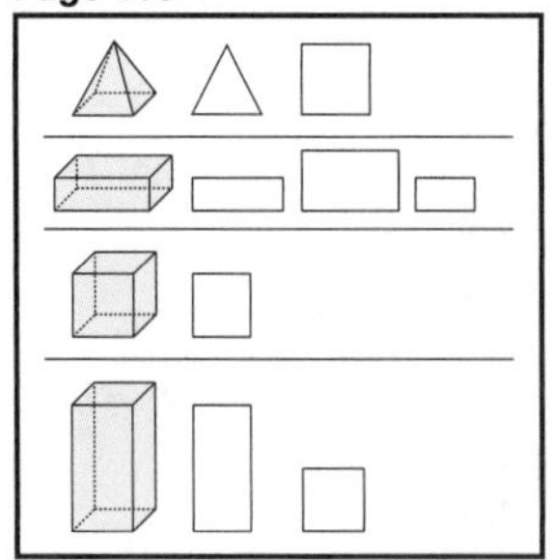

Page 109

Page 110

1

Page 111

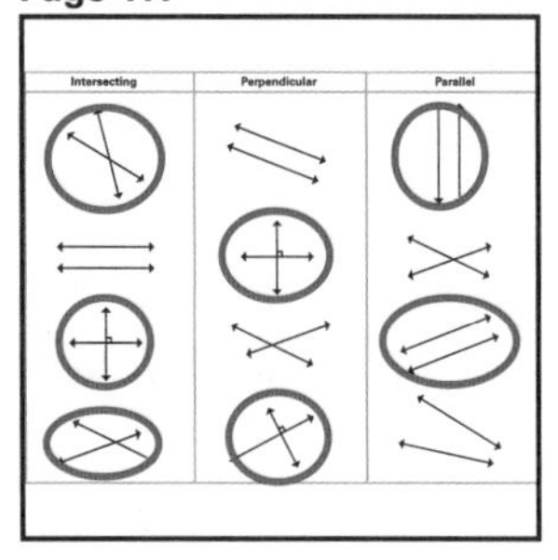

Page 112

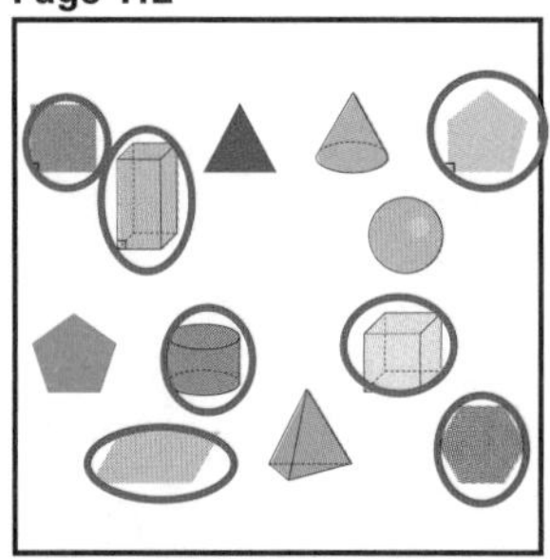

Page 113

1. turn 2. turn
3. slide 4. flip
5. flip 6. turn
7. turn 8. slide

Page 114

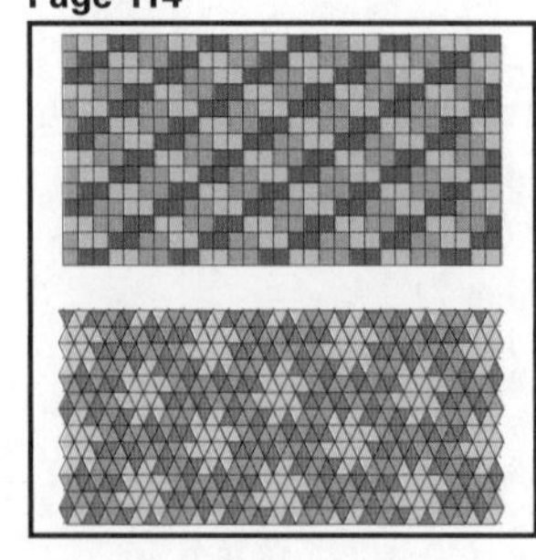

Page 115

1. hexagon
2. square pyramid
3. cube
4. rectangular prism
5. rectangle
6. pentagon
7. cylinder
8. heptagon
9. cone
10. nonagon
11. sphere
12. octagon

Page 116

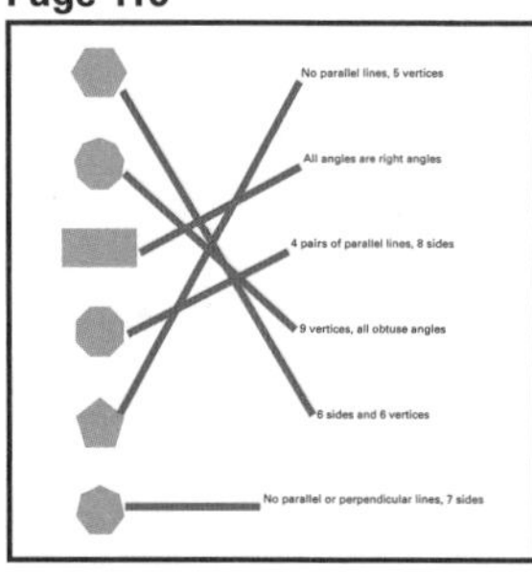

Page 117

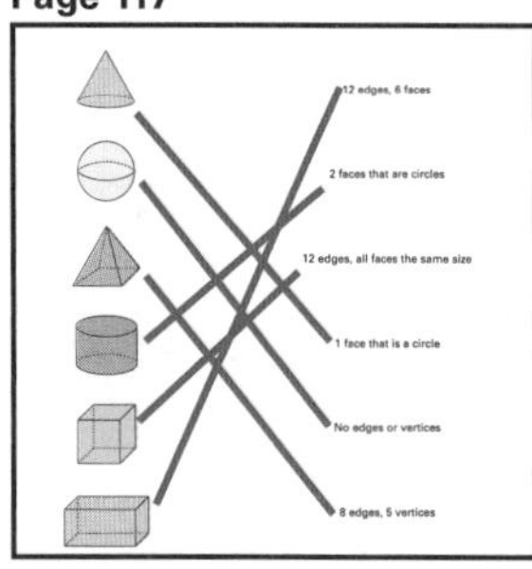

Page 118

1. right
2. acute
3. obtuse
4. acute
5. right
6. parallel
7. intersecting
8. intersecting, perpendicular
9. intersecting, perpendicular
10. parallel
11. intersecting
12. turn
13. flip
14. slide